A Short
Dictionary of
ASTROLOGY

A Short Dictionary of ASTROLOGY

MARYLEE BYTHERIVER

HARPER COLOPHON BOOKS
Harper & Row, Publishers
New York, Hagerstown, San Francisco, London

FIRST EDITION

Designed by Stephanie Winkler

ISBN: 0-06-090629-4

79 80 81 82 83 10 9 8 7 6 5 4 3 2 1

To Rebel, for helpful information
based on his practical experience and
personal knowledge of navigation.
And for his friendship.

Preface

A *Short Dictionary of Astrology* grew out of an editorial project to revise and update Llewellyn George's classical astrology textbook *The A to Z Horoscope Maker and Delineator,* first published in 1910. While working on the glossary of the new, revised edition, I realized the need for a brief, concise, but clearly written and illustrated dictionary of astrological terms. The present text was written to meet that need.

A *Short Dictionary of Astrology* is not meant to be an interpretive text, but merely a handy reference, particularly for the many professionals who are unsure of the astronomical background behind the horoscope, as well as for students of astrology and astronomy everywhere.

Special thanks go to Marne Purple for her critical comments and rave reviews.

Marylee Bytheriver, Ettersburg, California
August 1977

A Short
Dictionary of
ASTROLOGY

A

affinity. Attraction or similarity between planets, signs, houses, mundane events, or areas of life.

affliction. Unfavorable aspect. A debility. A planet is said to be afflicted when in square, conjunction, opposition, or quincunx to other planets or angular house cusps, or when in any aspect to Mars, Saturn, Uranus, or Pluto. An afflicted planet is said to be *impedited,* or *impeded.*

anareta. Destroyer. Traditionally the planet believed to correspond with the termination of life. Usually an afflicted malefic planet, in conjunction or adverse aspect to the *hyleg.*

angles. The four points of the chart, dividing it into quadrants. The angles are sensitive areas that lend emphasis to planets situated near them.
The Ascendant: eastern horizon, cusp of the First House, or Oriens.
The Descendant: western horizon, cusp of the Seventh House, or Occidens.
Immum Coeli (IC): north vertical, cusp of the Fourth House. Popularly called the *Nadir,* with which it sometimes corresponds. See *Nadir.*
The Midheaven: Medium Coeli (MC), south vertical, Zenith, cusp of the Tenth House, meridian.

angular houses. The strongest of the mundane houses, corresponding to the cardinal signs: First House (Aries); Fourth House (Cancer); Seventh House (Libra); and Tenth House (Capricorn).

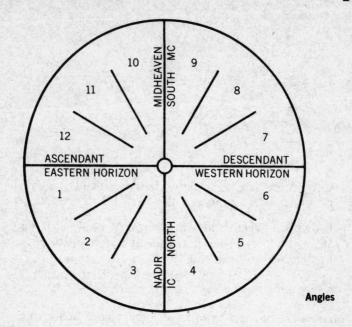

Angles

animoder of Tetrabiblos. A method of birth-time rectification, now obsolete, presented by Ptolemy. Sometimes referred to as the *sunrise indicator*.

antipathy. Inharmonious relations between planets that rule or are exalted in opposite signs. Also, conflict between the natal horoscopes of two people corresponding with the aversion they feel for one another.

aphelion. See *elongation*.

apogee. That place in the Moon's orbit at which it is farthest from the Earth. Opposite of *perigee*.

apparent motion. Motion of the planets as seen from the Earth, geocentrically measured, as opposed to the actual movement of the planets in their heliocentric, or Sun-centered, orbits.

application. The approach of one planet to another planet, house cusp, or exact aspect. The faster-moving planet *applies* to the aspect with the slower-moving planet. An applying aspect is

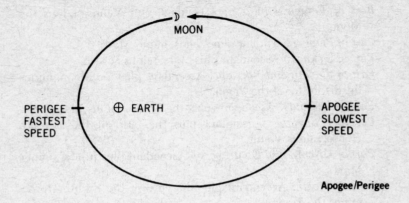

Apogee/Perigee

considered stronger than a separating aspect. Opposite of *separation*.

Arabian Parts. Points that are usually the arithmetic combination of two planets and the Ascendant, sometimes involving eclipses and house cusps. The only commonly used of the Arabian Parts is the *Part of Fortune*. See *Part of Fortune*.

Part of Life: Ascendant plus the Moon, minus the New or Full Moon nearest before birth.

Part of Understanding: Ascendant plus Mars, minus Mercury.

Part of Spirit: Ascendant plus the Sun, minus the Moon.

Part of Fortune: Ascendant plus the Moon, minus the Sun.

Part of Goods. Ascendant plus the cusp of the Second House, minus the lord of the Second House.

Part of Brethren: By day—Ascendant plus Jupiter, minus Saturn. By night—Ascendant plus Saturn, minus Jupiter.

Part of Love of Brethren: Ascendant plus Saturn, minus the Sun.

Part of the Father: Ascendant plus the Sun, minus Saturn.

Part of Fortune in Husbandry: Ascendant plus Saturn, minus Venus.

Part of Inheritance and Possessions: Ascendant plus the Moon, minus Saturn.

Part of Male Children: Ascendant plus Jupiter, minus the Moon.

Part of Female Children: Ascendant plus Venus, minus the Moon.

Part of Plays: Ascendant plus Venus, minus Mars.

Part of Sickness: Ascendant plus Mars, minus Saturn.

Part of Slavery and Bondage: Ascendant plus the Moon, minus the dispositor of the Moon.

Part of Servants: Ascendant plus the Moon, minus Mercury.

Part of Marriage: Ascendant plus the cusp of the Seventh House, minus Venus.

Part of Discord and Controversy: Ascendant plus Jupiter, minus Mars.

Part of Death: Ascendant plus the cusp of the Eighth House, minus the Moon.

Part of the Perilous and Most Dangerous Year: Ascendant plus the lord of the Eighth House, minus Saturn.

Part of Faith: Ascendant plus Mercury, minus the Moon.

Part of Journeys by Water: Ascendant plus 15° Cancer, minus Saturn.

Part of Travels by Land: Ascendant plus the cusp of the Ninth House, minus the lord of the Ninth House.

Part of the Mother: Ascendant plus the Moon, minus Venus.

Part of Nobility and Honor: By day—Ascendant plus 19° Aries, minus the Sun. By night—Ascendant plus 3° Taurus, minus the Moon.

Part of Sudden Advancement: Ascendant plus the Part of Fortune, minus Saturn (if Saturn is combust, substitute Jupiter).

Part of Magistry and Profession: Ascendant plus the Moon, minus Saturn.

Part of Merchandise: Ascendant plus the Part of Fortune, minus the Part of Spirit.

Part of Friends: Ascendant plus the Moon, minus Uranus.

Part of Honourable and Illustrious Acquaintance: By day—Ascendant plus the Sun, minus the Part of Fortune. By night—Ascendant plus the Part of Fortune, minus the Sun.

Part of Imprisonment, Sorrow, and Captivity: Ascendant plus the Part of Fortune, minus Neptune.

Part of Private Enemies: Ascendant plus the cusp of the Twelfth House, minus the lord of the Twelfth House.

arc. Distance measured along a circle. In astrology this refers to zodiacal longitude.

Ascendant. Rising Sign. Cusp of the First House. The degree of the zodiac on the eastern horizon at the time and place for which the horoscope is calculated. Each sign takes approximately two hours to rise above the horizon. Opposite of *Descendant.* See diagram under *Nadir.*

An *ascending planet,* or *rising planet,* is one that is between 12° above and 20° below the Ascendant. A planet is strengthened by this position. More generally, any planet in the eastern hemisphere between the Tenth House and the Fourth House.

The *ruling planet* is the planet that rules the sign of the Ascendant.

ascension. Due to the obliquity of the ecliptic, signs of long ascension require more time to rise above the horizon than do signs of short ascension.

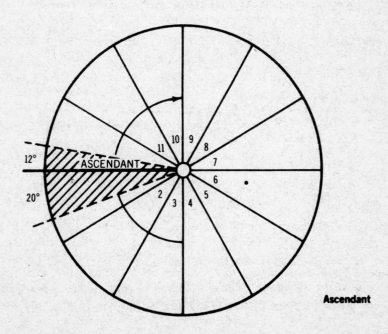

Ascendant

Signs of *long ascension* in the northern hemisphere: Cancer, Leo, Virgo, Libra, Scorpio, Sagittarius.

Signs of *short ascension* in the northern hemisphere: Capricorn, Aquarius, Pisces, Aries, Taurus, Gemini. These are the signs most often intercepted in a horoscope.

aspect. The angular relationship between planets, sensitive points, or house cusps in the horoscope. Lines drawn between the two points and the center of the chart, representing the Earth, form the angle of the aspect, which is equivalent to the number of degrees of arc between the two points. Parallels and conjunctions are also termed aspects, though no angles are formed.

Major aspects:

   ☌ *Conjunction,* 0°, same degree of longitude; a neutral aspect, its effect determined by the natures of the planets involved.

   ⚹ *Sextile,* 60°; a favorable aspect.

   □ *Square,* 90°; an adverse aspect. Also called a quadrate, quartile, or tetragonous aspect.

   △ *Trine,* 120°; a favorable aspect.

   ☍ *Opposition,* 180°; a neutral aspect, its effect determined by the natures of the planets involved.

Minor aspects:

   ⚺ *Semisextile,* 30°; slightly beneficial.

   ∠ *Semisquare,* 45°; slightly adverse. Also called a semiquadrate.

   # *Sesquiquadrate,* 135°; slightly adverse.

   ⚻ *Quincunx,* 150°; slightly adverse. Also called inconjunct, disjunct, or quadrasextile.

Seldom used aspects:

   ⌣ *Vigintile,* or semidecile, 18°; slightly favorable.

   √ *Quindecile,* 24°; slightly favorable.

   ⊥ *Decile,* or semiquintile, 36°; slightly favorable.

   Q *Quintile,* 72°; slightly favorable.

   ¥ *Tredecile,* 108°; slightly favorable.

   ± *Biquintile,* 144°; slightly favorable.

asteroids. Planetoids. Numerous small celestial bodies whose orbits lie between those of Mars and Jupiter. Though the as-

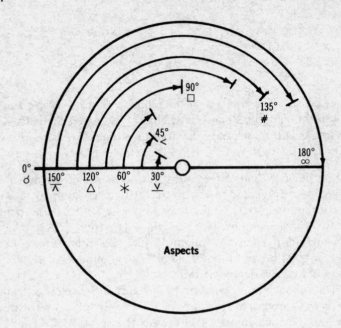

Aspects

teroids are not usually used in astrology, some attention is being paid to four of them: Ceres, Pallas, Juno, and Vesta. Another asteroid, *Lilith*, is used by some astrologers, and its zodiacal longitude is recorded in an ephemeris.

astro-twins. Two people with the same Sun Sign, Moon Sign, and Ascendant.

average daily motion. See *mean motion*.

B

benefics. Fortunes. Beneficial planets. Jupiter is traditionally called the *Greater Benefic*, while Venus is considered the *Lesser Benefic*.

birth time. The exact moment of the first indrawn breath of a baby.

C

cadent houses. The weakest of the mundane houses, corresponding to the mutable signs: Third House (Gemini); Sixth House (Virgo); Ninth House (Sagittarius); and Twelfth House (Pisces).

celestial equator. The extension of the Earth's equator out into space, perpendicular to the Earth's axis of rotation. Distance measured along the celestial equator, eastward from the point of the vernal equinox, is called *right ascension* (RA), which corresponds to terrestrial longitude. Right ascension is measured in hours: 24 hours to the circle of 360°, 4 minutes of right ascension for each degree of arc.

The distance of a planet north or south of the celestial equator is measured in *declination*, which corresponds to terrestrial latitude. The maximum declination of the Sun is 23°27′ N at 0°

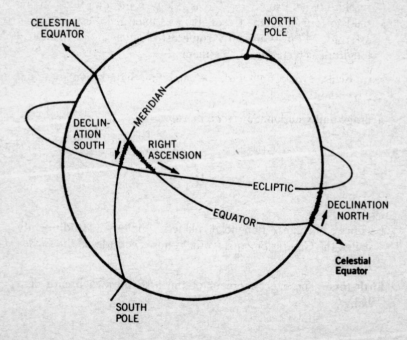

Cancer, and 23°27' S at 0° Capricorn. A planet situated on the celestial equator has no declination.

collection of light. A planet that is in aspect to two others that are not in themselves in aspect to each other. The *collector of light* acts as an intermediary. Used in horary astrology.

combust. Within 8°30' of zodiacal longitude of the Sun. The nature of the combust planet is combined with that of the Sun; either a weakening or a strengthening aspect. Mercury and Venus are the planets most often combust.

An *inferior conjunction* between Mercury or Venus and the Sun occurs when the planet comes between the Earth and the Sun, in retrograde motion.

A *superior conjunction* between Mercury or Venus and the Sun occurs when the planet is on the opposite side of the Sun from the Earth, in direct motion.

Under the Sun's beams is a traditional term used to indicate a planet that is within 17° of the Sun. Its influence is thereby weakened.

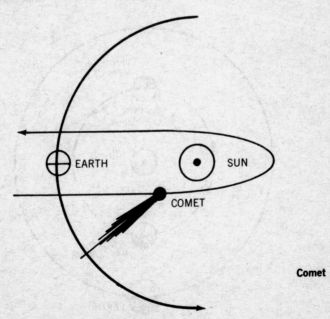

Comet

comets. Small luminous celestial bodies that circle the Sun on eccentric orbits. Comets often develop long fuzzy tails that point away from the Sun. Those with *elliptical orbits* return at regular intervals; but three-fourths of all comets have *parabolic orbits* (infinitely long ellipses), and these leave the solar system forever.

composite chart. See *midpoint*.

conjunction. A division of the zodiac by 1. An aspect that is exact at 0°, with a 10° orb for the Sun and Moon, 8° orb for the other planets. Two planets that are *conjunct* are located in the same sign; same house; and usually form the same aspects to the other planets. The conjunction strengthens the meaning of the planets; the effect is beneficial or detrimental depending on the nature of the planet involved. The strongest aspect.

constellation. Asterism. A group of stars named after a figure or pattern it is said to represent. Twelve constellations have the same names, but are no longer located in the same places, as the signs of the zodiac. This group of twelve constellations is

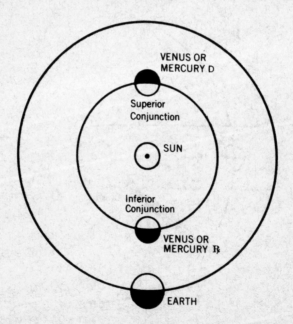

called the *sidereal zodiac,* fixed zodiac, or zodiac of the constellations.

converse directions. A system of directions that employs the symbolic reverse motion of the planets, movement contrary to the
natural course of the planets.

critical degrees. Mansions of the Moon. The subdivision of the
zodiac into twenty-eight parts of $12\frac{6}{7}°$ each, representing the
Moon's average daily motion, beginning with 0° Aries, divided
by sensitive points, the critical degrees, in the various signs.

Critical degrees of the *cardinal signs,* Aries, Cancer, Libra,
Capricorn: 0°, 13°, 26°.

Critical degrees of the *fixed signs,* Taurus, Leo, Scorpio,
Aquarius: 9°, 21°.

Critical degrees of the *mutable signs,* Gemini, Virgo, Sagittarius, Pisces: 4°, 17°.

culmination. The arrival of a planet at the Midheaven, by pro-
gression, direction, or transit. Also, the completion of an aspect.

D

daylight saving time. DST. Summer time. An artificial adjustment
of clock time, one hour ahead. One hour must be subtracted
from birth times recorded in standard time zones when daylight saving time is in effect, before the horoscope can be calculated. See *standard time.*

During World War I and World War II, daylight saving
time was in effect and was called *war time:* March 31, 1918, to
October 27, 1918; March 30, 1919, to October 26, 1919; and
February 9, 1942, to September 30, 1945.

debility. Positions and aspects that weaken the nature of the
planets. A planet is *debilitated* when adversely aspected, in a
cadent house, or in the sign of its detriment or fall. Opposite of
dignity.

decan. Decanate. Division of each of the signs into three equal
segments of 10° each. Each decan is ruled by a planet, though

controversy exists as to which planets rule which decans. Three different decan systems are given here as an example. Planetary rulers of each sign are marked in bold type.

Decan	Traditional Decans	Chaldean Decans	DuVlea Decans
0–9° Aries	**Mars**	**Mars**	Neptune
10–19°	Sun	Sun	**Mars**
20–29°	Jupiter	Venus	Venus
0–9° Taurus	**Venus**	Mercury	Mars
10–19°	Mercury	Moon	**Venus**
20–29°	Saturn	Saturn	Mercury
0–9° Gemini	**Mercury**	Jupiter	Venus
10–19°	Venus	Mars	**Mercury**
20–29°	Uranus	Sun	Moon
0–9° Cancer	**Moon**	Venus	Mercury
10–19°	Pluto	Mercury	**Moon**
20–29°	Neptune	**Moon**	Sun
0–9° Leo	**Sun**	Saturn	Moon
10–19°	Jupiter	Jupiter	**Sun**
20–29°	Mars	Mars	Mercury
0–9° Virgo	**Mercury**	Sun	Sun
10–19°	Saturn	Venus	**Mercury**
20–29°	Venus	**Mercury**	Venus
0–9° Libra	**Venus**	Moon	Mercury
10–19°	Uranus	Saturn	**Venus**
20–29°	Mercury	Jupiter	Pluto
0–9° Scorpio	**Pluto**	Mars	Venus
10–19°	Neptune	Sun	**Pluto**
20–29°	Moon	Venus	Jupiter
0–9° Sagittarius	**Jupiter**	Mercury	Pluto
10–19°	Mars	Moon	**Jupiter**
20–29°	Sun	Saturn	Saturn
0–9° Capricorn	**Saturn**	Jupiter	Jupiter
10–19°	Venus	Mars	**Saturn**
20–29°	Mercury	Sun	Uranus
0–9° Aquarius	**Uranus**	Venus	Saturn
10–19°	Mercury	Mercury	**Uranus**
20–29°	Venus	Moon	Neptune
0–9° Pisces	**Neptune**	Saturn	Uranus
10–19°	Moon	**Jupiter**	**Neptune**
20–29°	Pluto	Mars	Mars

declination. See *celestial equator.*

decreasing in light. Waning. Third and fourth quarters of the
Moon. A planet, particularly the Moon, during the half of its
cycle from opposition with the Sun to the next conjunction with
the Sun. Opposite of *increasing in light.* See diagram under
increasing in light.

degree. Degree of arc. One of the 360 divisions of a circle. The
circle of the zodiac is divided into 12 signs of 30° (degrees) each.
Each degree is made up of 60′ (minutes), and each minute is
made up of 60″ (seconds) of zodiacal longitude.

Descendant. Cusp of the Seventh House. The degree of the zodiac
on the western horizon at the time and place for which the
horoscope is calculated. Opposite of *Ascendant.*

A *descending planet* is one that is generally between the
Tenth House and the Fourth House in the western hemisphere.

detriment. The sign in which a planet is unfavorably placed; the
opposite sign of its own sign. Traditional rulerships are noted
in parentheses.

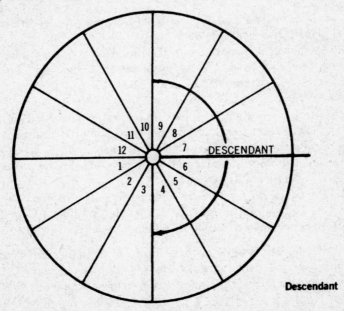

Descendant

Planet	Own Sign	Detriment
The Sun	Leo	Aquarius
The Moon	Cancer	Capricorn
Mercury	Gemini	Sagittarius
	Virgo	Pisces
Venus	Taurus	Scorpio
	Libra	Aries
Mars	Aries	Libra
	Scorpio	Taurus
Jupiter	Sagittarius	Gemini
	Pisces	Virgo
Saturn	Capricorn	Cancer
	Aquarius	Leo
Uranus	Aquarius	Leo
Neptune	Pisces	Virgo
Pluto	Scorpio	Taurus

dexter aspect. An aspect in which the faster-moving planet is ahead of, or has greater zodiacal longitude than, the aspected planet. This occurs when the aspecting planet is moving away from the slower-moving planet by direct motion, or toward it by retrograde motion. Also, loosely, a separating aspect. Opposite of *sinister aspect.*

dignity. Positions and aspects that strengthen the nature of the planet. Opposite of *debility.*

Accidental dignity refers to the planet's position by house, aspect, or motion. A planet is accidentally dignified when it is near the Midheaven, in an angular house, in its natural house, favorably aspected, swift in motion, direct in motion, or increasing in light. The most important accidental dignity occurs when a planet is near the Ascendant or Midheaven.

Essential dignity refers to the planet's position by sign. A planet is essentially dignified when it is in the sign it rules, or in the sign of its exaltation.

Domal dignity occurs when a planet is in its own sign.

Joy is an obsolete term for a favorable position for a planet, though not technically a position of dignity.

direct motion. Proper motion. Proceeding in the order of the signs from Aries toward Taurus, and so on. Denoted in the ephemeris by a "D." Opposite of *retrograde motion.*

directions. The aspects between planets or house cusps in a progressed horoscope and those in the natal horoscope, or between transiting and natal planets or house cusps. Also, loosely, *progressions*.
   Primary directions are aspects formed in a system of progressions that calculates one degree of forward motion for each of the planets in the natal horoscope for each year of life.

dispositor. The planet ruling the sign in which another planet is posited. A planet in its own sign has no dispositor. Used in horary astrology and sometimes in progressed or natal work.

diurnal. Belonging to the day. Above the horizon, between the Ascendant and Descendant in the southern hemisphere of the chart. Opposite of *nocturnal*.
   Diurnal arc refers to that portion of a planet's daily travel in which it is above the horizon. Opposite of *nocturnal arc*.

dwadachamsha. A subdivision of each sign into twelve equal parts of 2½° each. Used in Hindu astrology.

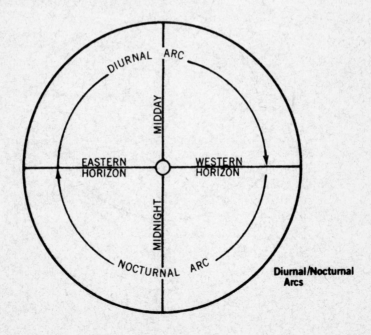

Diurnal/Nocturnal Arcs

E

Earth. Terra. The planet on which we live, represented as the center of the horoscope. The daily axial rotation of the Earth from west to east, its diurnal movement, produces the appearance of the Sun, Moon, and planets rising in the east and setting in the west. The Earth's annual revolution around the Sun produces the appearance of the Sun transiting through the signs. The Earth appears to be in the opposite sign of the Sun.

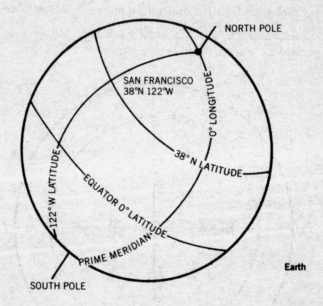

Earth

The *terrestrial equator* is a belt around the Earth, halfway between the north and south poles.

Geographical longitude is a measurement east or west along the Earth's equator, beginning with the prime meridian at Greenwich, England, designated 0°, and proceeding east and west to 180° on the opposite side of the Earth. Lines of longitude form circles perpendicular to the equator.

Geographical latitude is a measurement north or south of the Earth's equator, beginning with the equator itself, which is designated 0°, and proceeding north and south to 90°. Lines of latitude form circles parallel with the equator.

eclipse. A phenomenon that involves the Sun, Moon, and Earth. There are usually two to six eclipses a year. The sign and degree of an eclipse is important, particularly in mundane astrology.

A *solar eclipse* is produced by the Moon's passing between the Sun and the Earth, cutting off the light of the Sun. This occurs when a New Moon, the conjunction of the Sun and Moon, takes place near a lunar node.

A *lunar eclipse* is produced by the Earth's passing between the Sun and Moon, casting its shadow on the Moon. This occurs when a Full Moon, the opposition of the Sun and Moon, takes place near a lunar node.

An *occultation* is an eclipse of a planet or star by the Moon, which can occur only when the other body and the Moon are in the same degree of zodiacal longitude and declination.

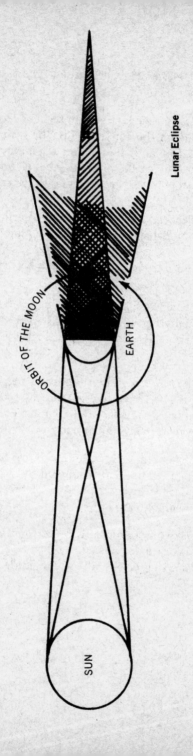

SUN

EARTH

ORBIT OF THE MOON

Lunar Eclipse

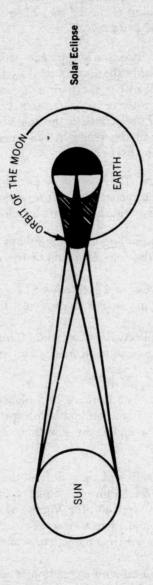

Immersion is the beginning of an eclipse or occultation. *Emersion* is the ending of the eclipse, when the planet comes out from under the Sun's rays.

ecliptic. *Via solis.* The Sun's apparent path around the Earth, which is in actuality the Earth's orbit extended out into space. So named because it is the path along which eclipses occur. The ecliptic forms the center of the zodiac.

The *obliquity of the ecliptic* is the angle between the plane of the ecliptic and the plane of the celestial equator, which varies according to the season.

electional astrology. The branch of astrology dealing with the selection of an auspicious time for a particular purpose. Sometimes considered a branch of horary astrology.

elements. Triplicities. Trigons. Four groups of three signs, each symbolized by the four elements of the ancients: fire, earth, air, and water.

Fire signs are active and enthusiastic: Aries, Leo, Sagittarius.

Earth signs are practical and cautious: Taurus, Virgo, Capricorn.

Air signs are intellectual and sociable: Gemini, Libra, Aquarius.

Water signs are emotional and sensitive: Cancer, Scorpio, Pisces.

elevation. Altitude. The distance of a planet above the horizon. The most elevated position in a horoscope is at the cusp of the Tenth House. The higher the elevation, the more powerful the planet.

elongation. The distance of a planet from the Sun, as viewed from the Earth. The maximum elongation of the inferior planets is 28° for Mercury and 48° for Venus. Mercury can therefore form only a conjunction and semisextile to the Sun; while Venus can form only a conjunction, semisextile, or semisquare to the Sun.

Aphelion is the maximum elongation of a planet; the point in its orbit at which it is farthest from the Sun.

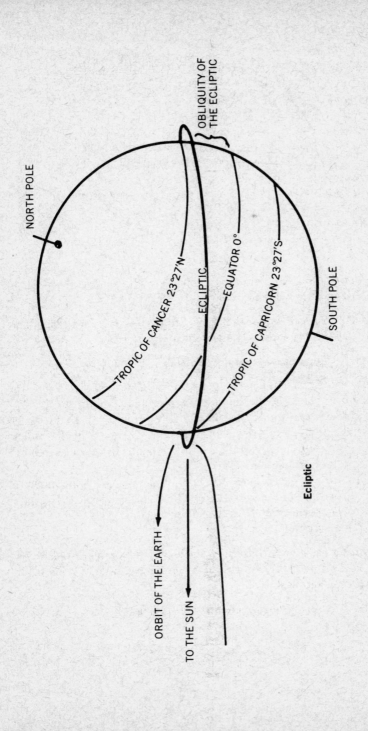

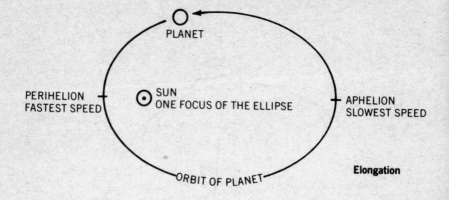

PLANET

PERIHELION
FASTEST SPEED

SUN
ONE FOCUS OF THE ELLIPSE

APHELION
SLOWEST SPEED

ORBIT OF PLANET

Elongation

Perihelion is the minimum elongation of a planet; the point in its orbit at which it is closest to the Sun.

ephemeris. A listing of the Sun's, Moon's, and planet's places and related information for astrological purposes.

equator. See *celestial equator; Earth.*

equinox. Equal night. The point in the Earth's orbit around the Sun at which the day and night are equal in length.

The *vernal equinox* occurs annually around March 21, when the Sun enters Aries, and marks the beginning of the zodiac. The ecliptic crosses the celestial equator from south to north at the vernal equinox.

The *autumnal equinox* occurs annually around September 21, when the Sun enters Libra. The ecliptic crosses the equator from north to south at the autumnal equinox.

See diagram under *solstice.*

esoteric astrology. Spiritual astrology. The branch of astrology dealing with the spiritual nature of the individual, his or her Karma and past lives.

exaltation. A sign in which a planet is favorably posited. Opposite of *fall.*

Planet	Exaltation	Fall
The Sun	Aries	Libra
The Moon	Taurus	Scorpio
Mercury	Virgo	Pisces
Venus	Pisces	Virgo
Mars	Capricorn	Cancer
Jupiter	Cancer	Capricorn
Saturn	Libra	Aries
Uranus	Scorpio	Taurus
Neptune	Cancer	Capricorn
Pluto	Pisces	Virgo

excitation. The influence of a transiting planetary aspect, bringing into effect a progressed aspect of similar nature.

extra-Saturnian planets. Modern planets. Outer planets. The three planets not visible to the naked eye, which lie outside the orbit of Saturn and were discovered in recent times: Uranus, discovered in 1781; Neptune, discovered in 1846; Pluto, discovered in 1930. See diagram under *solar system*.

Each of the extra-Saturnian planets is considered to be a *higher octave* of another planet: Uranus is a higher octave of Mercury; Neptune is a higher octave of Venus; Pluto is a higher octave of Mars.

F

face. Divisions of each of the signs into six equal segments of 5° each. Not used by modern astrologers.

fall. The sign in which a planet is unfavorably placed. The opposite sign of its exaltation. See listing under *exaltation*.

familiarity. Any kind of aspect or reception between the planets.

fertility. Classification of a sign according to productivity.

Fertile or *fruitful signs:* Cancer, Scorpio, Pisces. The fertile signs are good for planting when occupied by the Moon, and are indicators of offspring when occupying the cusps of the Fifth or Eleventh Houses.

Semifruitful or *moderately fertile signs:* Taurus, Libra, Capricorn.

Barren or *sterile signs:* Aries, Gemini, Leo, Virgo, Sagittarius, Aquarius. The barren signs are good for cultivation when occupied by the Moon, and are indicators of childlessness when occupying the cusps of the Fifth or Eleventh Houses.

fixed stars. The visible, seemingly immovable stars, as opposed to the Sun, Moon, and planets, which are traditionally called the *wandering stars.* The fixed stars do have a slight but measurable motion, Major visible stars in the northern hemisphere are sometimes taken into account in astrological work.

The following is a list of the major fixed stars, their zodiacal and constellational positions in 1965, and their traditional meanings:

Alpheratz, Andromeda's Head. 13° 54′ Aries, in the hair of Andromeda. Honor, intelligence, wealth.

Baten Kaitos, Whale's Belly. 21° 20′ Aries, in the body of the Whale. Misfortunes, accidents, assaults.

Mirach, The Loins. 29° 55′ Aries, in the girdle of Andromeda. Beauty, fame, brilliance, prosperous marriage.

Menkar, The Nose. 13° 47′ Taurus, in the jaw of the Whale. Disgrace, sickness, ruin.

Algol, Demon's Head. 25° 40′ Taurus, in Medusa's Head. The most evil star, violence.

Alcyone, The Hen. 28° 42′ Taurus, in the shoulder of the Bull. Violence, blindness, wantonness.

Alderbaran, The Follower. 9° 18′ Gemini, the Bull's left eye. Eloquence, opulence, power.

Rigel, The Foot. 16° 18′ Gemini, the left foot of Orion. Benevolence, fame, honor, wealth.

Bellatrix, Female Warrior, or Swiftly Destroying. 20° 26′ Gemini. Sudden dishonor, danger, blindness.

Capella, Little She-Goat. 21° 20′ Gemini, in the body of the Goat. Powerful friends, positions of trust.

Betelgeuze, Coming of the Branch. 28° 14′ Gemini, in the armpit of the Giant. Military genius, preferment, riches.

Sirius, The Dog Star. 13° 35′ Cancer, in the mouth of the Greater Dog. Faithfulness, danger from dogs.

Castor, A Ruler Yet to Come. 19° 35′ Cancer, in the head of the Northern Twin. Imprisonment, wounds, Occultism.

Pollux, A Heartless Judge. 22° 46′ Cancer, in the head of the Southern Twin. Crime, disgrace, danger from poison.

Procyon, Before the Dog. 25° 17′ Cancer, in the body of the Lesser Dog. Malevolence, injury from dogs.

North Asellus, Balaam's Ass. 6° 32′ Leo, in the body of the Crab.

South Asellus, Mare Ass. 7° 43′ Leo, in the body of the Crab. Combined meaning: slander, violence, burns, blindness.

Regulus, Little King, or Lion's Heart. 29° 20′ Leo, in the body of the Lion. Idealism, violence, command.

Spica, Wheat Ear of Virgo. 23° 19′ Libra, the wheat ear of Virgo. Fame, honor, wealth.

Arcturus, Bear Guard. 23° 43′ Libra, the left knee of the Herdsman. Fame, honor, water travel.

Antares, Rival of Mars. 9° 16′ Sagittarius, the Scorpion's Heart. Destruction, fatalism, headstrongness.

Altair, The Wounding. 1° 15′ Aquarius, in the neck of the Eagle. Confidence, courage, danger from reptiles.

Fomalhaut, Fishes Mouth. 3° 19′ Pisces, in the mouth of the Southern Fish. Immortality, inheritance, power.

Markab. 22° 59′ Pisces, in the buckler of the Ship. Eminence, wealth, danger from fevers.

focal point. A planet or aspect formation that is of primary importance within a horoscope.

fortunes. Beneficial planets. Jupiter and Venus are always called the fortunes. The Sun and Moon if favorably placed and aspected are also considered fortunate. Mercury and Neptune, being neutral, are fortunate when favorably placed and in favorable aspect to Venus or Jupiter.

frustration. A term used in horary astrology when one planet is applying to an aspect of another, but before the aspect culminates, a third planet, by its swifter motion, interposes by completing an aspect of its own, thus deflecting the influence of the slower-moving planet.

G

genethliacal astrology. Natal astrology. The branch of astrology dealing with the individual. The horoscope cast for the birth time of that individual, showing his or her life's potentials, is called a *natal horoscope, geniture, radix,* or *nativity.* The individual under consideration is called the *native.*

geocentric. Earth-centered. Astrology is a geocentric science, while astronomy is a heliocentric (Sun-centered) science.

great circle. Any circle, the plane of which passes through the center of the Earth, such as the celestial equator, the meridian, the ecliptic, and the lines of terrestrial longitude.

Greenwich Mean Time (GMT). Universal time. The time at the prime meridian of 0° longitude. The standard for navigation, astronomy, international communication, and astrology. Ephemerides are calculated for either noon or midnight Greenwich Mean Time.

H

heavy planets. The slower-moving planets, whose influence is considered more serious than that of the other planets: Jupiter, Saturn, Uranus, Neptune, Pluto. See diagram under *solar system.*

heliocentric. Sun-centered.

hemisphere. Half-circle. The division of the celestial vault into halves by the horizon and prime vertical. Also, the division of the horoscope into overlapping halves:
   The *eastern hemisphere* from the Midheaven through the Ascendant to the *Immum Coeli* (IC); the Tenth through Third Houses.

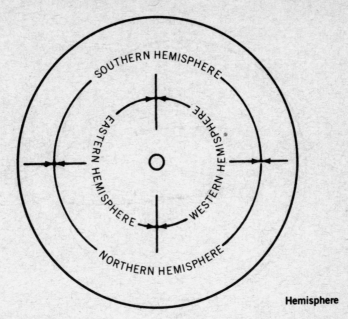

Hemisphere

The *northern hemisphere* from the Ascendant through the IC to the Descendant; the First through Sixth Houses.

The *western hemisphere* from the IC through the Descendant to the Midheaven; the Fourth through Ninth Houses.

The *southern hemisphere* from the Descendant through the Midheaven to the Ascendant; the Seventh through Twelfth Houses.

horary astrology. The branch of astrology in which a chart is calculated for the time a question is asked in order to ascertain the answer to that question.

horizon. The circle that separates the visible and invisible worlds. The *rational* or *true horizon* is the great circle that surrounds the observer, passing through the cardinal points. The poles of the rational horizon are defined by the Zenith overhead and the Nadir directly underneath the observer. A line between the Zenith and the Nadir would be perpendicular to the plane of the rational horizon.

The *celestial horizon* is the rational horizon extended infinitely

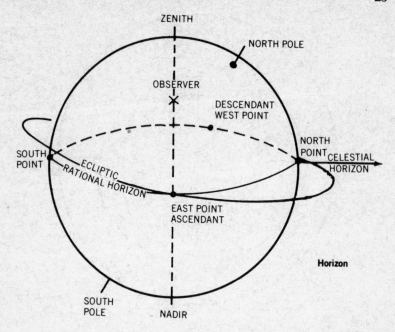

out into space. The intersection of the eastern horizon and the ecliptic determines the Ascendant. This is the east point of the chart. The intersection of the western horizon and the ecliptic determines the Descendant at the west point of the chart.

The *visible* or *apparent horizon* is the small area of the Earth visible with the naked eye. It is a parallel to the rational horizon.

horoscope. Map. Chart. Figure. A diagram of the positions of the planets, including the Sun and Moon, calculated for a specific time and place.

A *natural chart* is a horoscope with Aries on the Ascendant and no intersected signs.

A *solar chart* is a horoscope in which the planets' positions are calculated for noon Greenwich Mean Time (taken from a noon ephemeris) but with the Sun's longitude on the Ascendant. Used when the birth time is unknown.

Other common types of horoscopes:

In natal astrology: the *natal horoscope,* drawn for the birth of

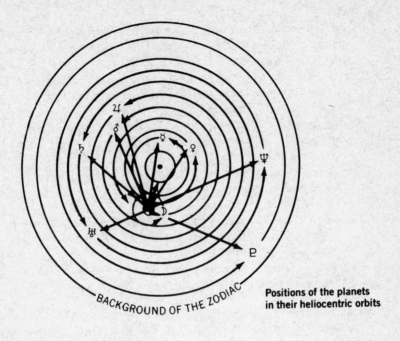

Positions of the planets in their heliocentric orbits

BACKGROUND OF THE ZODIAC

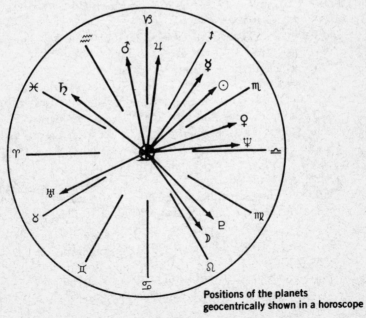

Positions of the planets geocentrically shown in a horoscope

an individual; the *transit chart*, showing the current positions of the planets; and the *progressed chart*, a symbolic representation of any year in the native's life.

In rectification work: the *prenatal chart*, drawn for the moment of conception; and the *rectified horoscope*, drawn for an estimated or assumed birth time.

In horary astrology: the *horary chart*, drawn to answer a question; and the *election chart*, to determine the best moment to undertake any activity.

In mundane astrology: the *lunation chart*, drawn for a New Moon; and the *ingress chart*, drawn for a planet's entry into a new sign.

A *synastry chart* compares two natal horoscopes, while a *composite chart* combines two charts through the use of midpoints.

A *locality chart*, or *relocation chart*, transposes the natal chart to the current or proposed place of residence.

house systems. There are twenty-two systems of dividing the astrological chart into the twelve houses, though only a few of these are in current use. Some of the systems currently popular include the following:

The Campanus System: Attributed to Johannes Campanus of Novara (1210–1296), astrologer to Pope Urban IV. A quadrant system dividing space trigonometrically into sections. The prime vertical, the great circle that passes through the east and west points of the horizon and through the Zenith and Nadir, is divided into six equal lunes. The degrees of the ecliptic that intersect these dividing lines are taken as the house cusps. The Ascendant is the cusp of the First House, and the Midheaven is the cusp of the Tenth House.

The Equal House System: One of the oldest systems, popularized in modern times by Charles E. O. Carter and Margaret Hone of the Faculty of Astrological Studies in London. A direct system; twelve houses of 30° each proceed from the degree of the Ascendant. The cusp of the Tenth House is the nonagesimal, 90° from the Ascendant/Descendant axis. The Midheaven, or degree of culmination, is drawn in the correct zodiacal longitude. It will appear to the right of the nonages-

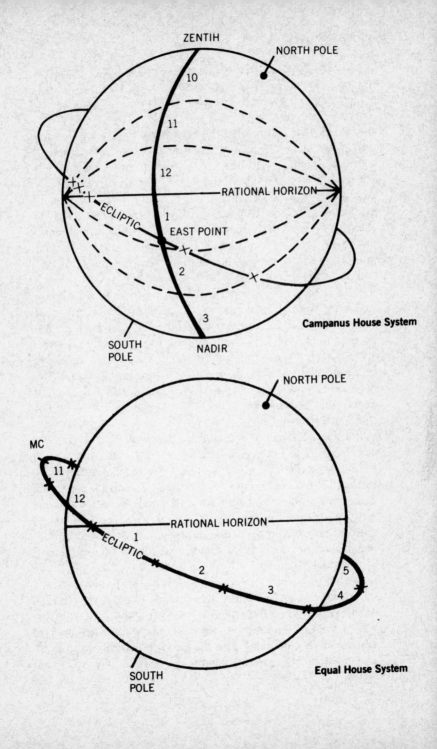

ZENTIH

NORTH POLE

10

11

12

RATIONAL HORIZON

ECLIPTIC

1

EAST POINT

2

3

SOUTH POLE

NADIR

Campanus House System

NORTH POLE

MC

11

12

RATIONAL HORIZON

ECLIPTIC

1

2

5

3

4

SOUTH POLE

Equal House System

imal, in the Eighth or Ninth House, when a sign of long ascension is rising. The Midheaven will appear to the left of the nonagesimal, in the Tenth or Eleventh House, when a sign of short ascension is rising.

The Koch System: Also called the Birthplace System or *Geburtsort Häuser.* Developed by Walter Koch (1895–1970), a German astrologer. An intersection system of technical complexity, though highly systematized in readily available tables.

The Placidus System: Developed by Placidus de Tito (1603–1668), a Spanish or Italian monk and professor of mathematics at the University of Padua. This system has been popular in modern times, mainly due to the easy accessibility of Placidian tables of houses. The only semiarc system, which divides time instead of space to form the houses. The house cusps are formed by taking the degrees of the ecliptic that have completed one-third or two-thirds of their own arc between the horizon and the lower meridian (nocturnal semiarc) and between the horizon and the upper meridian (diurnal semiarc). The degree on the horizon itself forms the Ascendant, the cusp of the First House; the culminating degree on the upper meridian is the Midheaven, the cusp of the Tenth House.

The Porphyry System: Developed by Porphyry (A.D. 233–303), a biographer of Pythagoras and Plotinus. A quadrant system sometimes called an equal system. The four quadrants are formed by the east point of the horizon and the Midheaven, and their opposites. These four unequal segments are divided into equal thirds to form the twelve houses. The houses within the first and third quadrants will all be equal in size, and the houses within the second and fourth quadrants will all be equal.

The Regiomontanus System. Developed by Regiomontanus (original name Johannes Müller) of Königsberg (1436–1476), professor of mathematics and astronomy at the University of Vienna. A quadrant system dividing space trigonometrically into sections. The celestial equator, an infinite extension of the earth's equator, is divided into six equal

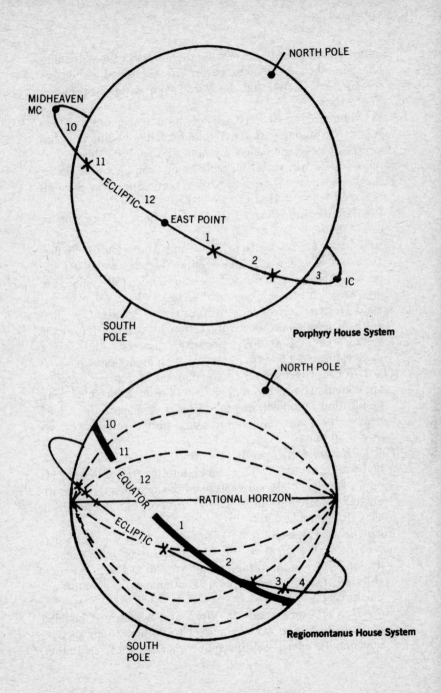

Porphyry House System

Regiomontanus House System

lunes. The degrees of the ecliptic that intersect these dividing
lines are taken as the house cusps. The Ascendant is the cusp
of the First House, and the Midheaven is the cusp of the
Tenth House.

houses. Mundane houses. Divisions of the horoscope into twelve
segments, beginning with the Ascendant. The dividing lines between the houses are called the *house cusps.* Each house corresponds to certain aspects of daily living or mundane affairs.

Houses above the horizon in the horoscope, the Seventh
through Twelfth Houses, are called the *day houses.* The
First House through the Sixth House, below the horizon, are
called the *night houses.*

First House: Corresponds to Aries and Mars. Classified fire,
angular. The creative/initiative trine. Represents the self, the
person, self-awareness, self-consciousness, self-confidence,
motivation, disposition, personality, ego.

Second House: Corresponds to Taurus and Venus. Classified
earth, succedent. The work/resources trine. Represents
values, feelings, stability, security, resources and assets,
money, income, possessions, means of obtaining desires.

Third House: Corresponds to Gemini and Mercury. Classified
air, cadent. The socio/communicative trine. Represents communications, intellect, mental dexterity, transportation, short
trips, education, sense impressions, public relations, news
media, siblings.

Fourth House: Corresponds to Cancer and the Moon. Classified water, angular. The personal/intuitive trine. Represents
home, family, childhood, maternal influence, memories, senti-
mentality, circumstances at the end of life, nationalism,
chauvinism, real estate.

Fifth House: Corresponds to Leo and the Sun. Classified fire,
succedent. The creative/initiative trine. Represents creativity, self-expression, pride, fame, pleasure, love, romance,
children, teaching, conception, amusements and entertain-
ment, risks.

Sixth House: Corresponds to Virgo and Mercury. Classified
earth, cadent. The work/resources trine. Represents service,
dependents, work, self-discipline, health, diet, sanitation,

morals, modesty, the military, civil service, public health, crops.

Seventh House: Corresponds to Libra and Venus. Classified air, angular. The socio/communicative trine. Represents relationships, partnerships, social pursuits, marriage, one's personality reflected in others, law, judgments.

Eighth House: Corresponds to Scorpio and Pluto. Classified water, succedent. The personal/intuitive trine. Represents transformation, regeneration, rebirth, death, legacies, inheritance, sex, Magick, the occult, other people's money, joint investments.

Ninth House: Corresponds to Sagittarius and Jupiter. Classified fire, cadent. The creative/initiative trine. Represents higher mind activities, philosophy, religion, advanced education, foreign travel, abstract reasoning, maturation, experience, publishing.

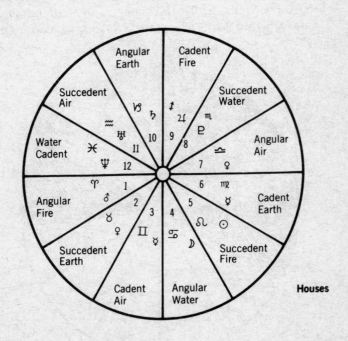

Houses

Tenth House: Corresponds to Capricorn and Saturn. Classified earth, angular. The work/resources trine. Represents career, business, public reputation, respect, authority, the establishment, paternal influences, future success.

Eleventh House: Corresponds to Aquarius and Uranus. Classified air, succedent. The socio/communicative trine. Represents friends, organizations, peer-group pressure, goals, ideals, objectives, politics, social sciences, reform movements, electronics, physics.

Twelfth House: Corresponds to Pisces and Neptune. Classified water, cadent. The personal/intuitive trine. Represents spiritual attainment, initiation, secrets, privacy, retirement, institutions, self-sacrifice, hidden enemies, past secrets, subconscious.

hyleg. Giver of life. A planet located in particular zones in the horoscope concerned with longevity: 25° into the Twelfth House to 25° into the First House; 25° into the Sixth House to 25° into the Seventh House; 25° into the Eighth House, through the Ninth and Tenth Houses, to 25° into the Eleventh House. A planet that is hyleg is called the *apheta* or the *prorogator.*

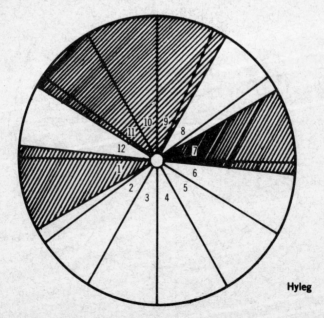

Hyleg

I

Immum Coeli (IC). Bottom of the heavens. Cusp of the Fourth House, the lowest point on the ecliptic at which it intersects the meridian below the horizon. The northern point of the horoscope. Opposite the *Midheaven*. Also, loosely, the *Nadir*, which is opposite the Zenith. See also diagram under *Nadir*.

increasing in light. Waxing. First and second quarters of the Moon. A planet, particularly the Moon, during the half of its cycle from conjunction to opposition with the Sun. Applies to superior planets only. Opposite of *decreasing in light*.

inferior conjunction. See *combust*.

inferior planets. Those planets, Mercury and Venus, whose orbits are between the Earth and the Sun. See diagram under *solar system*.

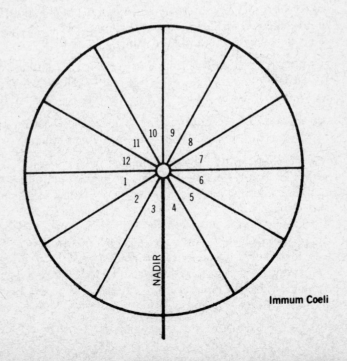

Immum Coeli

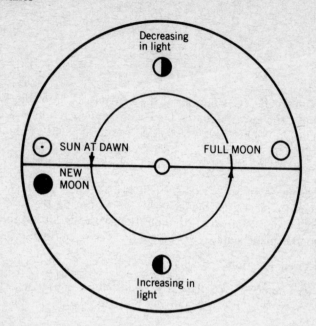

infortunes. Malefic planets. Mars, Saturn, and Uranus are always called the infortunes. Mercury and Neptune, being neutral, are infortunate when afflicted by position or aspect. Pluto is sometimes considered an infortunate planet.

ingress. The entrance of a planet into a sign. Also, loosely applied to the Sun's entrance into the four cardinal signs at the solstices and equinoxes.

inner planets. The swifter-moving planets most active in the horoscope: the Sun, the Moon, Mercury, Venus, Mars.

intercepted sign. A sign that is contained wholly within a house: it does not appear on any house cusp. Intercepted signs appear only in the horoscope; there are never any intercepted signs in the zodiac.

In the northern hemisphere the signs most often intercepted are those of short ascension: Capricorn, Aquarius, Pisces, Aries, Taurus, Gemini. Intercepted signs appear more frequently in extreme north or south latitudes, and less frequently near the equator.

L

latitude. See *Earth; zodiac.*

lights. Luminaries. The Sun and Moon, as distinguished from the planets. The Sun is the *Greater Light,* or *Greater Luminary;* the Moon is the *Lesser Light,* or *Lesser Luminary.*

Lilith. See *asteroids.*

local time. Sun time. True local time. Solar time. The actual time at a location within a time zone, adjusted to compensate for the standardization of time throughout the zone. Noon local time is always the time when the Sun transits the meridian of a particular place.

logarithms. Proportional logarithms. Tables of representational numbers that simplify the processes of multiplication and division in addition and subtraction. Used in horoscope calculation.

longitude. See *Earth; zodiac.*

lunar phases. The Moon's cycle from New Moon to New Moon is divided into four phases, each lasting about seven days.
First quarter: From the conjunction (New Moon) to the square of the Sun and Moon. During the first half of this phase, when the Moon is between 0° and 45° ahead of the Sun, it is called the *Crescent Moon.* A waxing phase.
Second quarter: From the square to the opposition (Full Moon) of the Sun and Moon. During the second half of this phase, when the Moon is between 135° and 180° ahead of the Sun, it is called the *Gibbous Moon.* A waxing phase.
Third quarter: From the opposition (Full Moon) to the square of the Sun and Moon. During the last half of this phase, when the Moon is between 135° and 90° behind the Sun, the Moon is called the *Disseminating Moon.* A waning phase.
Fourth quarter: From the square to the conjunction (New Moon) of the Sun and Moon. During the last half of this phase, when the Moon is between 45° and 0° behind the Sun, the Moon is called the *Balsamic Moon.* A waning phase.

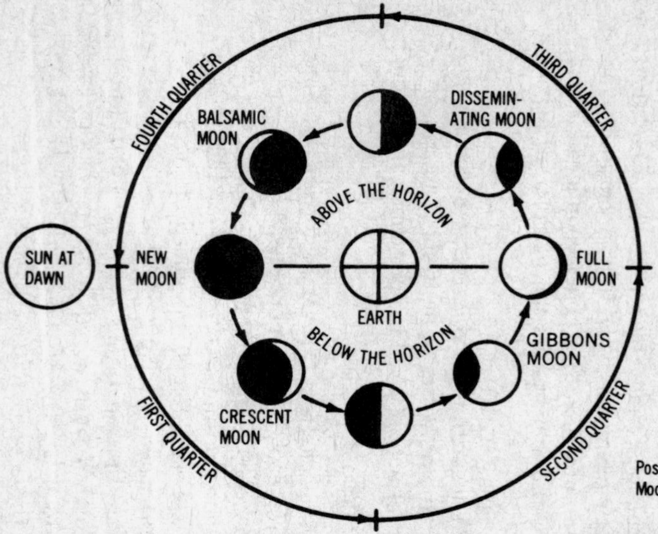

Lunar Phases

THIRD QUARTER

SECOND QUARTER

FULL MOON

DISSEMIN-
ATING MOON

GIBBONS
MOON

ABOVE THE HORIZON

EARTH

BELOW THE HORIZON

BALSAMIC
MOON

CRESCENT
MOON

NEW MOON

TO THE SUN

FOURTH QUARTER

FIRST QUARTER

SUN AT
DAWN

Position of the
Moon at dawn

Fourth Quarter
Begins

Full Moon

Second Quarter
Begins

New Moon

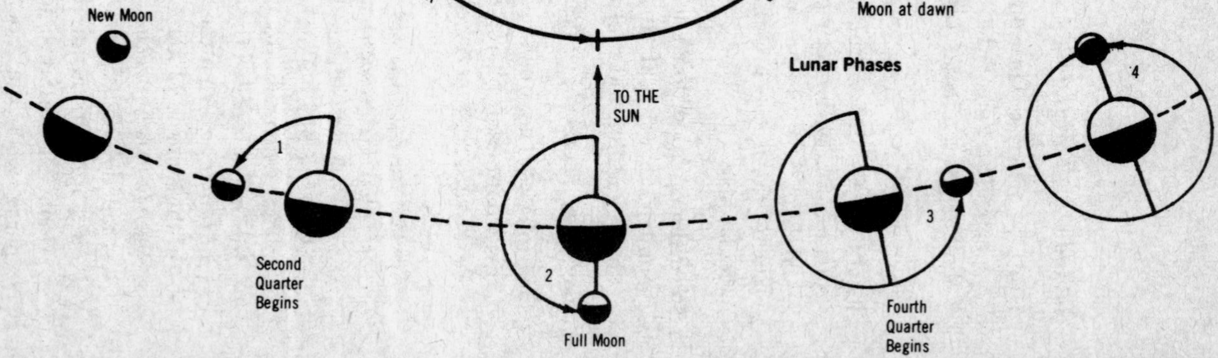

Combined Motion of the Earth and Moon

lunation. Lunar period. New Moon. Synodical lunation. The period from one New Moon, the conjunction of the Sun and Moon, until the next New Moon: 29 days, 12 hours, 44 minutes. Also, a chart drawn up for the time of the New Moon, used in mundane astrology. Also, loosely, the occurrence of the New Moon itself.

Neomenia is a traditional term for the New Moon, especially near the vernal equinox.

An *embolismic lunation* occurs each month when the Moon and Sun are in the same angular relationship, or lunar phase, as they were in the natal horoscope. The embolismic lunation coincides with a woman's astrological fertile period and is the basis of astrological birth control.

lune. A portion of a sphere contained between two great semi-circles. Each of the twelve lunes of the sphere represents one of the twelve houses.

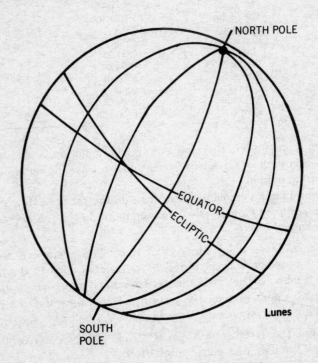

M

malefics. Evil planets. Saturn is traditionally called the *Greater Malefic*, while Mars is considered the *Lesser Malefic*.

Mansions of the Moon. See *critical degrees*.

matutine. Stars or planets that rise before the Sun in the morning, particularly the Moon (fourth quarter), Mercury, or Venus (oriental) when they appear in the morning. Opposite of *vespertine*.

mean motion. Average daily motion. Rate of motion. The average motion of any planet during a twenty-four-hour period:

Planet	Mean Motion
The Sun	0°59′08″
The Moon	13°10′36″
Mercury	1°23′
Venus	1°12′
Mars	0°31′27″
Jupiter	0°04′59″
Saturn	0°02′01″
Uranus	0°00′42″
Neptune	0°00′24″
Pluto	0°00′15″

When traveling less than the average daily motion, a planet is *slow in motion*, or *slow in course*. When traveling more, it is *swift in motion*.

When a planet is moving faster than on the previous day, it is *increasing in motion;* when moving more slowly, it is *decreasing in motion*.

mean time. Mean solar time. Civil time. The average day of twenty-four hours as measured by our clocks. Due to the uneven rotation of the earth, the day from noon to noon is slightly unequal, depending on the season. Mean time refers to the agreed-upon average in standard use.

meridian. The North–South Great Circle. A great circle that passes through the south point of the horizon, through the

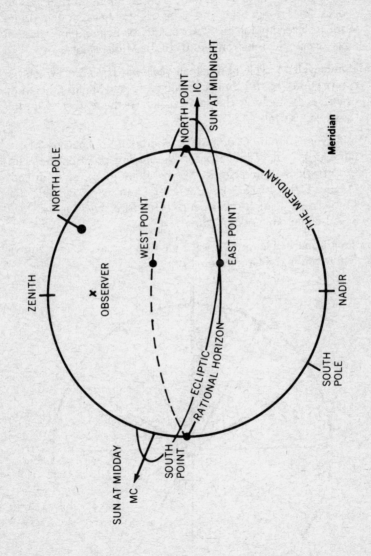

Meridian

Zenith directly overhead, and through the north point of the horizon, and under the Earth, through the Nadir. The Sun crosses the meridian at midday. The meridian corresponds to geographical longitude, and is at right angles to the prime vertical. Every point on earth has its own meridian. Also, in a horoscope, the line from the IC to the Midheaven.

Metonic cycle. A cycle of nineteen years, at the end of which the conjunctions of the Sun and Moon (New Moons) begin to occur successively in the same places in the zodiac as during the previous cycle.

Midheaven. *Medium Coeli* (MC). Middle of the heavens. Meridian. Cusp of the Tenth House. The highest point on the ecliptic, at which it intersects the meridian that passes directly overhead the place for which the horoscope is cast. The southern point of the horoscope. Opposite the *Immum Coeli*. See also diagram under *Nadir*.

midnight mark. The mean local time at any place that is equivalent to midnight, Greenwich, England.

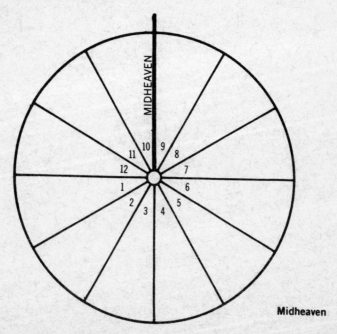

Midheaven

midpoint. Half-sum. A point equally distant from two planets or house cusps. In the horoscope there are actually two midpoints for each pair of planets: one on the shorter arc, usually used in astrology; and one on the longer arc, its opposite.

A *composite chart* is a chart using the midpoints between pairs of planets in two or more natal horoscopes, interpreted as an indication of the relationship between the people involved.

modes. Quadruplicities. Qualities. Three groups of four signs, one of each element.

Cardinal signs are active and powerful: Aries, Cancer, Libra, Capricorn.

Fixed signs are organized and resistant to change; Taurus, Leo, Scorpio, Aquarius.

Mutable or *common signs* are adaptable and resourceful: Gemini, Virgo, Sagittarius, Pisces.

mundane astrology. Political astrology, Judicial astrology. State astrology. The branch of astrology dealing with affairs of the world and collective activities of people.

mutual reception. See *reception.*

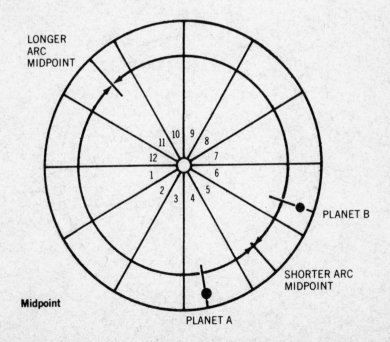

Midpoint

N

Nadir. A point opposite the Zenith. Often incorrectly applied to the *Immum Coeli* (IC). The IC, being on the ecliptic, is the point opposite the Midheaven.

navamsas. A subdivision of the zodiac into nine equal parts of 40° each. Used in Hindu astrology.

nocturnal. Belonging to the night. Below the horizon, between the Descendant and the Ascendant in the northern hemisphere of the chart. Opposite of *diurnal.*
Nocturnal arc refers to the portion of a planet's daily travel in which it is below the horizon. Opposite of *diurnal arc.* See diagram under *diurnal.*

nodes. The points at which the orbit of the Moon or other planet crosses the ecliptic. The Sun has no nodes, as its orbit defines the ecliptic. The planets' nodes change very slightly in a cen-

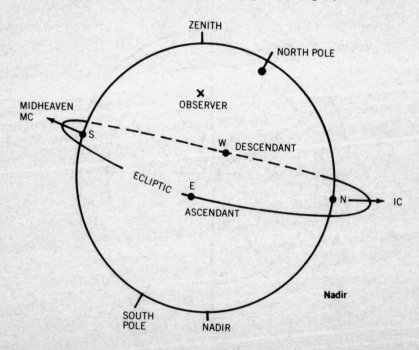

tury. The Moon's nodes, however, retrograde along the ecliptic about 3′ per day. The *ascending node,* or *north node,* occurs where the planet's orbit passes through the ecliptic from south to north latitude. The *descending node* occurs where the planet's orbit passes through the ecliptic from north to south.

Dragon's Head. Caput Draconis. The Moon's north node. The point at which the orbit of the Moon crosses the ecliptic from south to north latitude. A beneficial point. Opposite the Dragon's Tail.

Dragon's Tail. Cauda Draconis. The Moon's south node. The point opposite the Moon's north node. An unfavorable point.

nonagesimal. The point 90° from the ascending point; the highest point on the ecliptic above the horizon. The cusp of the Tenth House in the Equal House System.

noon mark. The mean local time at any place that is equivalent to noon at Greenwich, England.

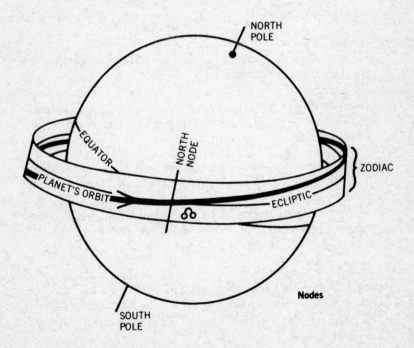

Nodes

O

occidental. Western. A planet that rises and sets after the Sun. Also, the western hemisphere of the chart, from the Tenth House cusp through the Descendant to the Fourth House cusp. Opposite of *oriental*.

Mercury is occidental during its *Epimethean cycle,* beginning with its superior conjunction with the Sun, moving direct until its maximum distance from the Sun, then moving retrograde until it reaches its inferior conjunction with the Sun.

Venus is occidental when it is *Hesperus,* the *evening star,* beginning with its superior conjunction with the Sun, moving direct until its maximum distance from the Sun, then moving retrograde until it reaches its inferior conjunction with the Sun.

occultation. See *eclipse.*

opposition. A division of the zodiac by 2. An aspect that is exact at 180°, with a 10° orb for the Sun and Moon, 8° orb for the other planets. Two planets are in opposition when they are in opposite signs; different elements (fire/air or earth/water); same quadruplicity; same polarity. The natures of the planets involved can either balance or compete with each other, in a manner similar to *conjunction.* A major aspect.

orb. The range of zodiacal longitude within which the influence of a planet or aspect operates, varying in size according to the specific planet and aspect. An aspect that is exact, has no orb, is called an exact aspect, or *partile aspect.* It has the strongest influence. An aspect that is not exact, yet still within the orb of influence, is called a wide aspect, or *platic aspect.* Its influence is weakened.

oriental. Eastern. A planet that rises and sets before the Sun. Also, the eastern hemisphere of the chart, from the Fourth House cusp through the Ascendant to the Tenth House cusp. Opposite of *occidental.*

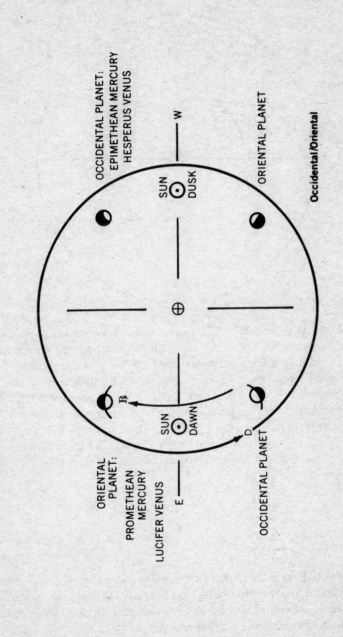

Occidental/Oriental

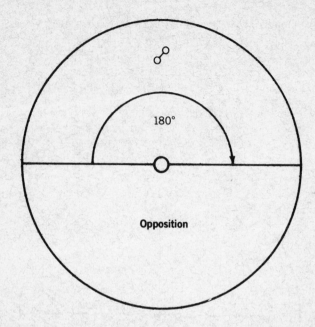

180°

Opposition

Mercury is oriental during its *Promethean cycle,* beginning
with its inferior conjunction with the Sun, moving retrograde
until its maximum distance from the Sun, then moving direct
until it reaches its superior conjunction to the Sun.

Venus is oriental when it is *Lucifer,* the Bearer of Light, the
morning star, beginning with its inferior conjunction with
the Sun, moving retrograde until its maximum distance from
the Sun, then moving direct until it reaches its superior conjunction with the Sun. See diagram under *occidental.*

P

parallel. Two planets that are equally distant from the celestial
equator, having the same declination, either both north or
both south, or one north and the other south. Similar in meaning to *conjunction.* A minor aspect.

A *mundane parallel* occurs when two planets are equally distant from any angle in the horoscope. The planets are then *antiscia*.

A *rapt parallel* occurs when two planets are equally distant from the meridian, at the point of Midheaven.

Part of Fortune. *Pars Fortuna.* A point that is equally distant from the Ascendant as the Moon is from the Sun in longitude. An indicator of the lunar phase. If the Part of Fortune is conjunct the Ascendant, the native was born under a New Moon; if the Part of Fortune is conjunct the *Immum Coeli* (IC), the Moon was just beginning the second quarter at the time of birth; if the Part of Fortune is opposite the Ascendant, the Sun was opposite the Moon (Full Moon); if the Part of Fortune is conjunct the Midheaven, the Moon was just beginning the fourth quarter.

The Part of Fortune is found by adding the longitude of the Moon to the longitude of the Ascendant and subtracting the longitude of the Sun from the sum. A mildly favorable point. The only commonly used of the many Arabian Parts.

peregrine. Foreign. The position of a planet in a sign in which it is neither dignified nor debilitated, nor in the same element as the sign it rules. No planet is peregrine if it is in mutual reception with another. Used in horary astrology.

Planet	Peregrine in
The Sun	Taurus, Gemini, Cancer, Virgo, Scorpio, Capricorn, Pisces
The Moon	Aries, Gemini, Leo, Virgo, Libra, Sagittarius, Aquarius
Mercury	Aries, Cancer, Leo, Scorpio
Venus	Cancer, Leo, Sagittarius
Mars	Gemini, Virgo, Aquarius
Jupiter	Taurus, Libra, Aquarius
Saturn	Virgo, Sagitarrius, Pisces
Uranus	Aries, Cancer, Virgo, Sagittarius, Capricorn, Pisces
Neptune	Aries, Taurus, Gemini, Leo, Libra, Sagittarius, Aquarius
Pluto	Aries, Gemini, Leo, Libra, Sagittarius, Capricorn, Aquarius

perigee. The place in the Moon's orbit at which it is closest to the Earth. Opposite of *apogee*. See diagram under *apogee*.

perihelion. See *elongation*.

planetary hours. A system in which the various hours of the day are ruled by the seven visible planets, beginning at sunrise with the planet that rules that day of the week. The time between sunrise and sunset is divided into twelve equal segments, as is the time between sunset and sunrise.

Planet	Day of the Week
The Sun	Sunday
The Moon	Monday
Mars	Tuesday
Mercury	Wednesday
Jupiter	Thursday
Venus	Friday
Saturn	Saturday

planetary rulership. The sign in which a planet is most harmoniously placed. Originally the seven visible planets were assigned to two signs, with the exception of the Sun and Moon, which were given one sign. The discovery of the three extra-Saturnian planets upset the symmetry and provided new corulers for Scorpio (Pluto), Aquarius (Uranus), and Pisces (Neptune).

Sign	Ruling Planet	Sign
Leo	The Sun	Leo
Cancer	The Moon	Cancer
Gemini	Mercury	Virgo
Taurus	Venus	Libra
Aries	Mars	Scorpio
Pisces	Jupiter	Sagittarius
Aquarius	Saturn	Capricorn
Aquarius	Uranus	Aquarius
Pisces	Neptune	Pisces
Scorpio	Pluto	Scorpio

planets. In astrology the term *planets* commonly refers to the Sun, the star at the center of our solar system; the Moon, the Earth's satellite; and the eight planets excluding the Earth.

⊙ *The Sun:* Corresponds to Leo and the Fifth House. Classified hot, dry, masculine. Relates to orange, gold (metal), Sunday, Tarot Key XIX: the Sun. Represents the personality, ego, creativity (masculine), vitality, self-expression, luxury, power, authority, wealth.

☽ *The Moon:* Corresponds to Cancer and the Fourth House. Classified cold, moist, feminine. Relates to yellow, violet, silver (metal), Monday, Tarot Key II: the High Priestess. Represents response, emotions, feelings, fluctuation, moods, changes, the Mother, conception, maternal instincts, intuition, sensitivity.

☿ *Mercury:* Corresponds to Gemini and the Third House, and Virgo and the Sixth House. Classified cold, moist, neutral. Relates to azure blue, orange, quicksilver (metal), Wednesday, Tarot Key I: the Magician. Represents intellect, mentality, communications, everyday activities, transportation, education, the sense of sight.

♀ *Venus:* Corresponds to Taurus and the Second House, and Libra and the Seventh House. Classified feminine. Relates to turquoise, pink, green, copper (metal), Friday, Tarot Key III: the Empress. Represents relationships, love, partnerships, pleasure, creativity (feminine), harmony, peace, unity, art, the sense of touch.

♂ *Mars:* Corresponds to Aries and the First House, and, traditionally, Scorpio and the Eighth House. Classified hot, dry, masculine. Relates to red, iron, Tuesday, Tarot Key XVI: the Tower. Represents energy, initiatory impulses, activity, courage, strength, physical health, violence, sex, competitiveness, impulsiveness, foolhardiness, the sense of taste.

♃ *Jupiter:* Corresponds to Sagittarius and the Ninth House and traditionally, Pisces and the Twelfth House. Classified hot, moist, masculine. Relates to green, royal blue, purple, tin, Thursday, Tarot Key X: the Wheel of Fortune. Represents expansion, success, benefit, new experiences, advanced education, growth, maturation, foreign travel, religion, philosophy, the sense of smell.

♄ *Saturn:* Corresponds to Capricorn and the Tenth House, and, traditionally, Aquarius and the Eleventh House. Classified cold, dry, masculine. Relates to black, lead, Saturday, Tarot Key XXI: the World. Represents limitation, definition, boundaries, authority, established power, the Father, business, profession, conservatism, caution, practicality, the sense of hearing.

♅ *Uranus:* Corresponds to Aquarius and the Eleventh House.

Classified cold, dry, masculine. Relates to checks, plaids, uranium, Tarot Key 0: the Fool. Represents rebellion, revolution, disruptive change, inspiration, originality, politics, social reform, brotherhood, communality, the future, the sense of clairvoyance (inner sight). A higher octave of Mercury.

Ψ *Neptune:* Corresponds to Pisces and the Twelfth House. Classified cold, moist, neutral. Relates to sea-green, gases, neptunium, Tarot Key XII: the Hanged Man. Represents idealism, impressionability, vagueness, psychic receptivity, escapism, sensitivity, adaptability, spiritualism, dreams, visions, drugs, secrets, the sense of psychometry (inner touch). A higher octave of Venus.

♇, ♀ *Pluto:* Corresponds to Scorpio and the Eighth House. Classified masculine. Relates to bloodred, plutonium, Tarot Key XX: Judgment. Represents regeneration, reincarnation, transformation, death, destruction, decay, waste, recycling, renewal, the underworld, crime, Sex Magick. A higher octave of Mars.

polarity. The division of the signs and planets into positive, masculine, creative, dry, yang, and their opposites, negative, feminine, receptive, moist, yin.

The *positive signs* are the fire and air signs: Aries, Gemini, Leo, Libra, Sagittarius, Aquarius. The *positive planets* are the Sun, Mars, Jupiter, Saturn, Uranus, and Pluto.

The *negative signs* are the earth and water signs: Taurus, Cancer, Virgo, Scorpio, Capricorn, Pisces. The *negative planets* are the Moon and Venus.

Mercury and Neptune are considered *neutral* or *convertible planets,* being either positive or negative, depending on whether they are located in positive or negative signs.

Gender emphasis refers to the predominance of masculine or feminine elements in the horoscope.

precession of the equinoxes. The gradual movement of the vernal equinox point, 0° Aries, which marks the beginning of the tropical zodiac, backward in relation to the constellations that define the sidereal zodiac, at the rate of approximately 50″ of zodiacal longitude per year, or one sign every 2,150 years, determining the *astrological ages,* or *great months.*

The equinox point regressed into Pisces at the birth of Christ, the beginning of the Age of Pisces. The *Age of Aquarius* would then begin around A.D. 2150.

The arc representing the gap between the tropical zodiac and the sidereal zodiac is called the *ayanamsa*, and was approximately 24°25′ in 1975.

prenatal epoch. The astrological moment of conception, about nine months before birth, but not necessarily coinciding with the actual time of biological conception. Used in rectification work.

prime vertical. The East–West Great Circle. A great circle that passes through the east point of the horizon, through the Zenith overhead, through the west point of the horizon, and under the Earth through the Nadir. It is perpendicular to the meridian.

progressions. The symbolic movement of the planets after birth, representing the future of the native. Usually refers to *secondary progressions*.

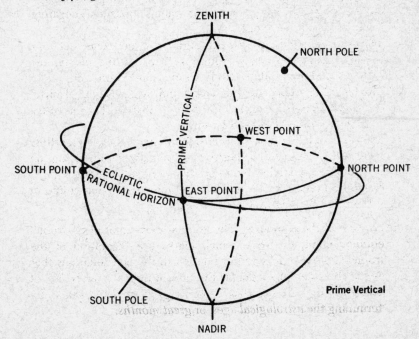

Prime Vertical

Secondary progressions is the most popular system of progressions, in which each day after birth represents the corresponding year in the life of the native

promittor. Promisor. A planet or configuration that signifies certain events. Used in horary astrology.

Q

quadrants. The four quarters of the chart. Also, the four seasons of the year.

quadrature. The Moon's dichotomies; changes, phases, or quarters. Also, a square aspect to the Sun, as occurs when the Moon is at the beginning of the second quarter or the beginning of the fourth quarter.

quadruplicities. See *modes.*

quincunx. An aspect that is exact at 150°, with an 8° orb for the Sun and Moon, a 6° orb for the other planets. Two planets in quincunx are in different elements (fire/earth, earth/air, air/water, or water/fire); different quadruplicities (cardinal/mutable, mutable/fixed, fixed/cardinal); different polarity (positive/negative). The effect is similar to the *square,* causing tension and conflict within the native. A minor aspect.

yod: Two planets sextile each other, both quincunx a third planet, form a *yod,* or *finger of God.* The *yod* involves each of the three quadruplicities, and three of the four elements. The planets in sextile are of the same polarity; and the third, of the opposite polarity. A stressful aspect, scattering the energies or focusing them through the leg of the *yod.*

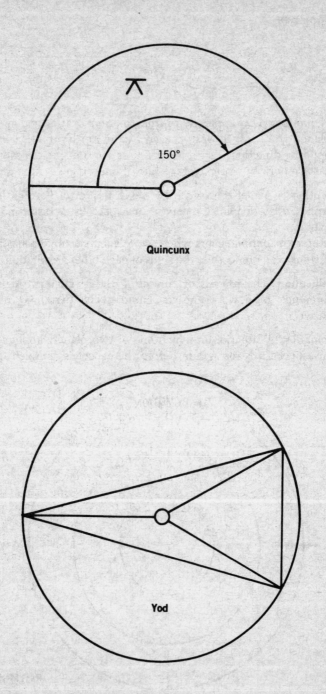

Quincunx

Yod

R

rapt motion. The apparent diurnal motion of the zodiac and planets from east to west, caused by the Earth's rotation in the opposite direction. This motion causes the signs to rise over the eastern horizon at the average rate of one sign every two hours.

reception. A planet is *received* by the dispositor of the sign it occupies. Also, a planet receives an aspect by a faster-moving planet.
Mutual reception occurs when two planets occupy each other's signs or, more loosely, the signs of each other's exaltation.

rectification. The process of correcting the given birth time by reference to known events or characteristics pertaining to the native.

refranation. A situation in which one of two planets applying to an aspect turns retrograde before the aspect is complete. The

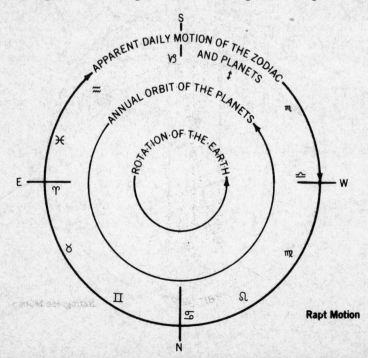

Rapt Motion

retrograde planet is said to *refrain,* signifying that the effect indicated by the approaching aspect will not materialize. Used in horary astrology.

relocation chart. Locality chart. A horoscope cast for a change of residence by putting the natal positions of the planets into houses calculated for the new location.

retrograde motion. Apparent backward motion of a planet in the reverse order of the signs, from Aries toward Pisces, and so on. Denoted in the ephemeris by the symbol ℞. Retrograde motion is an illusion caused by the relative motion of the Earth and the other planets in their elliptical orbits. Opposite of *direct motion.*
The Sun and Moon are never retrograde. The superior planets are retrograde around the time of their opposition to the Sun, once a year. The inferior planets are always retrograde at their inferior conjunction to the Sun; that is, when they are between the Earth and the Sun.

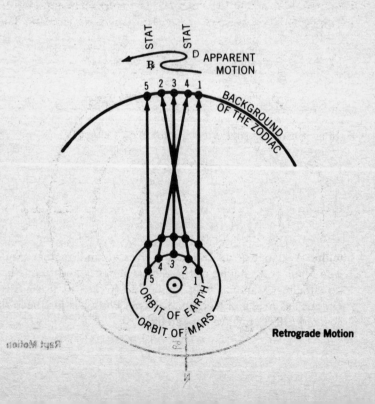

Retrograde Motion

Planet	Retrograde Period	Direct Period
Mercury	20–24 days	94 days
Venus	40–43 days	542 days
Mars	58–81 days	710 days
Jupiter	120 days	
Saturn	140 days	
Uranus	155 days	
Neptune	157 days	
Pluto	160 days	

return. The return of the Sun, Moon, or other planet to its natal place. Also, a chart erected for such an event. Used in progressed work.

revolution. Any orbit or movement describing a circle or ellipse. The revolutions of the planets are measured in time taken to circle the zodiac.

Planet	Revolution
The Sun	1 year
The Moon	28 days
Mercury	1 year
Venus	1 year
Mars	2 years
Jupiter	12 years
Saturn	28–30 years
Uranus	84 years
Neptune	165 years
Pluto	250 years

right ascension. See *celestial equator*.

S

satellite. A planet or moon that revolves around another planet. The Moon is a satellite of the Earth. Mercury and Venus have no satellites; Mars has two; Jupiter has twelve; Saturn has ten; Uranus has five; and Neptune has two. Pluto has just been discovered (1978) to have one satellite.

semisextile. A division of the zodiac by 12. An aspect that is exact at 30°, with a 4° orb for the Sun and Moon, a 2° orb for the other planets. Two planets in semisextile are in neighboring signs; different elements (fire/earth, earth/air, air/water, water/fire); different quadruplicities (cardinal/mutable, mutable/fixed, fixed/cardinal); opposite polarity (positive/negative). A slightly stressful aspect. A minor aspect.

separation. The movement of a planet away from another planet, house cusp, or exact aspect. The faster-moving planet *separates* from the aspect with the slower-moving planet and is called the *separator.* A separating aspect is considered weaker than an applying aspect. In horary astrology a separating aspect corresponds to events just past. Opposite of *application.*

sextile. A division of the zodiac by 6. An aspect that is exact at 60°, with an 8° orb for the Sun and Moon, a 6° orb for the other planets. Two planets in sextile are one sign apart; in different elements (fire/air, earth/water); different quadruplicities (cardinal/mutable, mutable/fixed, fixed/cardinal); same

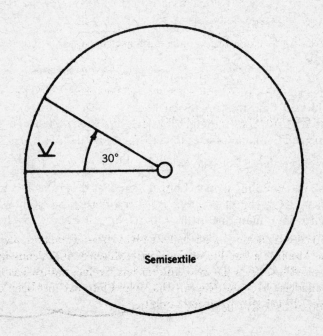

Semisextile

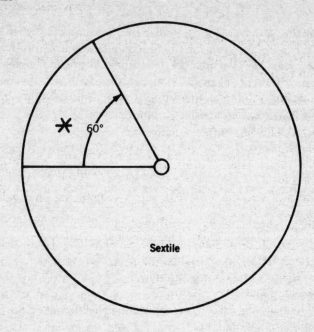

Sextile

polarity. A slightly favorable aspect, denoting creativity and opportunity. A minor aspect.

sidereal time. Time based on the interval between two successive transits of 0° Aries over the upper meridian. One *sidereal day* equals 23 hours, 56 minutes, 4.09 seconds of clock time—which is divided into 24 sidereal hours of 60 sidereal minutes each. Sidereal time for Greenwich Mean Time noon or for Greenwich Mean Time midnight for each day is given in the ephemeris and is 4 minutes later than the previous day.

sidereal zodiac. See *constellation*.

significator. Ruling planet. Lord. The planet that rules the Ascendant. Also, the planet that rules the horoscope, section of a horoscope, mundane event, area of life, or question in horary astrology. Also, the planet that rules a sign.

The *cosignificator*, or *coruler*, is a secondary or equal significator of a horoscope, section of a horoscope, mundane event, or area of life. Also, the traditional rulers of the signs now ruled by the extra-Saturnian planets: Mars is coruler of

Scorpio together with Pluto; Jupiter is coruler of Pisces together with Neptune; Saturn is coruler of Aquarius together with Uranus.

signs, classifications. The twelve signs of the zodiac are classified according to various categories, as follows:

Air signs: Gemini, Libra, Aquarius.

Barren signs: Aries, Gemini, Leo, Virgo, Sagittarius, Aquarius.

Bestial signs: Aries, Taurus, Leo, Capricorn, the last half of Sagittarius.

Bicorporeal, or *double-bodied, signs:* Gemini, the first half of Sagittarius, Pisces.

Cardinal signs: Aries, Cancer, Libra, Capricorn.

Cold signs: Taurus, Cancer, Virgo, Scorpio, Capricorn, Pisces.

Dry signs: Aries, Leo, Virgo, Sagittarius, Capricorn.

Earth signs: Taurus, Virgo, Capricorn.

Equinoctial signs: Aries, Libra.

Feminine or *negative signs:* Taurus, Cancer, Virgo, Scorpio, Capricorn, Pisces.

Fire signs: Aries, Leo, Sagittarius.

Fixed signs: Taurus, Leo, Scorpio, Aquarius.

Fruitful signs: Cancer, Scorpio, Pisces.

Hot signs: Aries, Leo, Libra, Sagittarius.

Human signs: Gemini, Virgo, the first half of Sagittarius, Aquarius.

Long ascension, in northern latitudes: Cancer, Leo, Virgo, Libra, Scorpio, Sagittarius.

Masculine or positive signs: Aries, Gemini, Leo, Libra, Sagittarius, Aquarius.

Moist signs: Taurus, Gemini, Cancer, Libra, Aquarius, Pisces.

Mutable, or *common, signs:* Gemini, Virgo, Sagittarius, Pisces.

Mute signs: Cancer, Scorpio, Pisces.

Northern signs: Aries, Taurus, Gemini, Cancer, Leo, Virgo.

Semifruitful signs: Taurus, Libra, Capricorn.

Short ascension, in northern latitudes: Capricorn, Aquarius, Pisces, Aries, Taurus, Gemini.

Southern signs: Libra, Scorpio, Sagittarius, Capricorn, Aquarius, Pisces.

Tropical signs: Cancer, Capricorn.

Voice signs: Gemini, Virgo, Libra, Sagittarius, Aquarius.
Water signs: Cancer, Scorpio, Pisces.

signs of the zodiac. The twelve 30° divisions of the zodiac, beginning with the position of the Sun at the vernal equinox around March 21, 0° Aries.

♈ *Aries:* the Ram. The Sun is in Aries from March 21 to April 20. Relates to the First House, red, iron, the head and face, Tuesday, Tarot Key IV: the Emperor. Ruled by Mars. Aries traits: energetic, impulsive, passionate, eager, impatient, courageous.

♉ *Taurus:* the Bull. The Sun is in Taurus from April 20 to May 21. Relates to the Second House, pink and turquoise, copper (metal), the throat, Friday, Tarot Key V: the Hierophant. Ruled by Venus. Taurus traits: patient, sensual, cautious, practical, resourceful, thoughtful, stubborn.

♊ *Gemini:* the Twins. The Sun is in Gemini from May 21 to June 21. Relates to the Third House, silver (color), mercury (metal), the nervous system, arms and lungs, Wednesday, Tarot Key VI: the Lovers. Ruled by Mercury. Gemini traits: intelligent, communicative, diverse, dexterous, inconsistent.

♋ *Cancer:* the Crab. The Sun is in Cancer from June 21 to July 23. Relates to the Fourth House, gray, silver (metal), the breasts and stomach, Monday, Tarot Key VII: the Chariot. Ruled by the Moon. Cancer traits: emotional, maternal, moody, sympathetic, changeable, possessive.

♌ *Leo:* the Lion. The Sun is in Leo from July 23 to August 23. Relates to the Fifth House, gold (color) and scarlet, gold (metal), the heart and back, Sunday, Tarot Key VIII: Strength. Ruled by the Sun. Leo traits: forceful, dominating, generous, gregarious, affectionate, arrogant.

♍ *Virgo:* the Virgin. The Sun is in Virgo from August 23 to September 22. Relates to the Sixth House, navy and gray, mercury (metal), the bowels, Wednesday, Tarot Key IX: the Hermit. Ruled by Mercury. Virgo traits: analytical, nervous, serious, discreet, thoughtful, critical.

♎ *Libra:* the Scales. The Sun is in Libra from September 22 to October 23. Relates to the Seventh House, blue-green, copper (metal), the lower back and kidneys, Friday, Tarot Key XI: Justice. Ruled by Venus. Libra traits: sociable, artistic, gracious, indecisive, honest, compassionate.

♏ *Scorpio:* the Scorpion or Eagle. The Sun is in Scorpio from October 23 to November 22. Relates to the Eighth House, bloodred, iron, the sex organs, Tuesday, Tarot Key XIII: Death. Ruled by Pluto; coruled by Mars. Scorpio traits: intense, secretive, mystical, shrewd, violent, sexual, loyal.

♐ *Sagittarius:* the Archer. The Sun is in Sagittarius from November 22 to December 22. Relates to the Ninth House, purple and green, tin, the hips and thighs, Thursday, Tarot Key XIV: Temperance. Ruled by Jupiter. Sagittarius traits: independent, cheerful, blunt, physical, sincere, insensitive, romantic.

♑ *Capricorn:* the Goat. The Sun is in Capricorn from December 22 to January 20. Relates to the Tenth House, black and brown, lead, the knees, bones and skin, Saturday, Tarot Key XV: the Devil. Ruled by Saturn. Capricorn traits: conservative, dignified, prudent, ambitious, pessimistic, slow.

♒ *Aquarius:* the Water Bearer. The Sun is in Aquarius from January 20 to February 18. Relates to the Eleventh House, checks and stripes, uranium, the calves and ankles, Saturday, Tarot Key XVII: the Star. Ruled by Uranus; coruled by Saturn. Aquarius traits: rebellious, humanitarian, idealistic, detached, original, erratic.

♓ *Pisces:* the Fish. The Sun is in Pisces from February 18 to March 21. Relates to the Twelfth House, sea-green and lavender, tin, the feet, Thursday, Tarot Key XVIII: the Moon. Pisces traits: adaptable, naive, psychic, unstable, sensitive, escapist, impressionable.

singleton. A planet standing alone in a quadrant or hemisphere of the horoscope. A singleton planet often acts as the focal point of the chart.

sinister aspect. An aspect in which a faster-moving planet is behind, or has lesser zodiacal longitude than, an aspected planet. This occurs when the aspecting planet is moving toward the slower-moving planet in direct motion, or moving away from

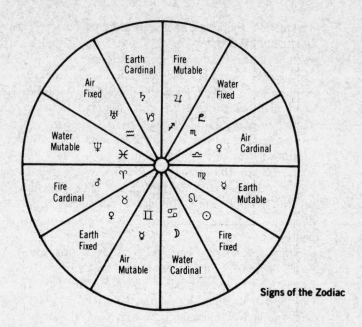

Signs of the Zodiac

it in retrograde motion. Also, loosely, an applying aspect. Opposite of a *dexter aspect*.

solar system. The Sun with the group of celestial bodies that revolve around it. This group comprises 9 planets, attended by 32 satellites; about 1,200 asteroids, which revolve in an orbit between Mars and Jupiter; and also comets and meteors. In order of increasing distance from the Sun they are:

Mercury	Jupiter and 12 moons
Venus	Saturn and 10 moons
Earth and the Moon	Uranus and 5 moons
Mars and 2 moons	Neptune and 2 moons
asteroids	Pluto and 1 moon

solstice. Standing still. The point in the Earth's orbit around the Sun in which the ecliptic reaches its maximum obliquity.

The *summer solstice* occurs annually around June 22, when the Sun enters Cancer at 23°27′ N declination, its highest point in the northern hemisphere. The longest day of the year.

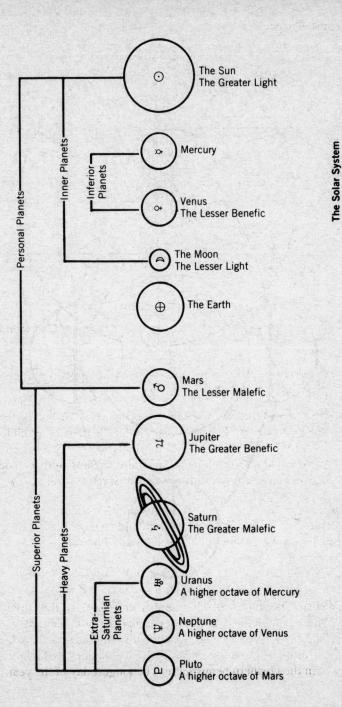

The Sun
The Greater Light

Mercury

Venus
The Lesser Benefic

The Moon
The Lesser Light

The Earth

Mars
The Lesser Malefic

Jupiter
The Greater Benefic

Saturn
The Greater Malefic

Uranus
A higher octave of Mercury

Neptune
A higher octave of Venus

Pluto
A higher octave of Mars

Personal Planets

Inner Planets

Inferior Planets

Superior Planets

Heavy Planets

Extra-Saturnian Planets

The Solar System

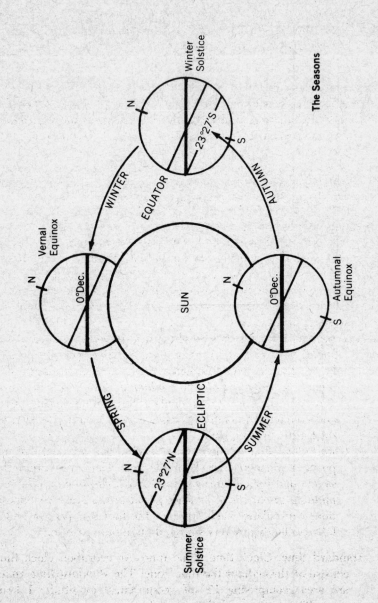

The Seasons

Winter Solstice

N

23°27′S

S

WINTER

EQUATOR

AUTUMN

Vernal Equinox

N

0°Dec.

SUN

N

0°Dec.

Autumnal Equinox

S

SPRING

ECLIPTIC

SUMMER

N

23°27′N

S

Summer Solstice

The *winter solstice* occurs annually around December 22, when the Sun enters Capricorn at 23°27′ S declination, its lowest point in the northern hemisphere. The shortest day of the year.

speculum. A table appended to a horoscope, containing the principal data concerning the horoscope, such as longitude, latitude, declination, right ascension, meridian distance, semiarc, and ascensional difference of the planets. Used in primary directions (see *directions*).

A *speculum of aspects* is a table made to show every degree in a horoscope that may be in aspect to the natal planetary positions. Used in transit work.

square. A division of the zodiac by 4. An aspect that is exact at 90°, with a 10° orb for the Sun and Moon, an 8° orb for the other planets. Two planets square each other are in different elements (fire/earth, earth/air, air/water, water/fire); the same quadruplicity; opposite polarity (positive/negative). The natures of the planets will be conflicting, causing tension and stress. A major aspect.

T-square: Two planets opposed each other, with a third planet square both of them, form a T-square. All of the planets will be in the same quadruplicity, containing three of the elements: *cardinal T-square, mutable T-square,* or *fixed T-square.* This is a most difficult formation, causing stress and conflict. The pattern is unbalanced, focusing tension on the fourth, missing point.

Grand cross: Four planets square each other—two pairs of opposition planets—in each of the four elements within the same quadruplicity form a grand cross: *cardinal grand cross, mutable grand cross,* or *fixed grand cross.* The two oppositions can balance each other, or the four squares can be totally conflicting. A very strong, though rare, pattern.

standard time. Clock time. Zone time. Agreed-upon clock time consistent throughout the time zone. The *standard time zones* are areas comprising 15° of geographical longitude, 1 hour apart. Time zones and their meridians west of Greenwich follow:

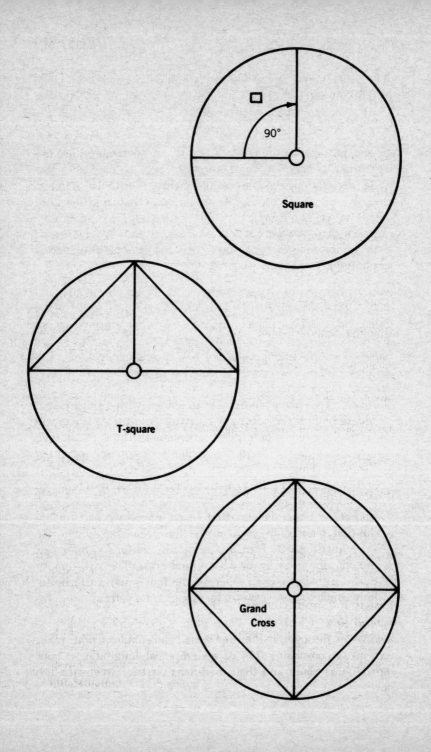

Greenwich Mean Time (GMT)	0° longitude, 0 hours
West Africa Time (WAT)	15° W longitude, 1 hour earlier
Azores Time (AT)	30° W longitude, 2 hours earlier
Brazil Standard Time (BST)	45° W longitude, 3 hours earlier
Newfoundland Time (NFT)	52°30′ W longitude, 3½ hours earlier
Greenwich Mean Time (GMT)	0° longitude, 0 hours
Atlantic Standard Time (AST)	60° W longitude, 4 hours earlier
Eastern Standard Time (EST)	75° W longitude, 5 hours earlier
Central Standard Time (CST)	90° W longitude, 6 hours earlier
Mountain Standard Time (MST)	105° W longitude, 7 hours earlier
Pacific Standard Time (PST)	120° W longitude, 8 hours earlier
Yukon Standard Time (YST)	135° W longitude, 9 hours earlier
Alaska-Hawaii Standard Time (AHST)	150° W longitude, 10 hours earlier
Bering Time (BT)	165° W longitude, 11 hours earlier
International Date Line, West (IDLW)	180° W longitude, 12 hours earlier

Time zones and their meridians east of Greenwich follow:

Greenwich Mean Time (GMT)	0° longitude, 0 hours
Central European Time (CET)	15° E longitude, 1 hour later
Eastern European Time (EET)/ USSR Zone 1	30° E longitude, 2 hours later
Baghdad Time (BT)/USSR Zone 2	45° E longitude, 3 hours later
Iran Time (IT)	52°30′ E longitude, 3½ hours later

USSR Zone 3	60° E longitude, 4 hours later
USSR Zone 4	75° E longitude, 5 hours later
Indian Standard Time (IST)	82°30′ E longitude, 5½ hours later
USSR Zone 5	90° E longitude, 6 hours later
North Sumatra Time (NST)	97°30′ E longitude, 6½ hours later
South Sumatra Time (SST)/USSR Zone 6	105° E longitude, 7 hours later
Java Time (JT)	112°30′ E longitude, 7½ hours later
China Coast Time (CCT)/USSR Zone 7	120° E longitude, 8 hours later
Moluccas Time (MT)	127°30′ E longitude, 8½ hours later
Japanese Standard Time (JST)/USSR Zone 8	135° E longitude, 9 hours later
South Australia Standard Time (SAST)	142°30′ E longitude, 9½ hours later
Guam Standard Time (GST)/USSR Zone 9	150° E longitude, 10 hours later
USSR Zone 10	165° E longitude, 11 hours later
New Zealand Time (NZT)	180° E longitude, 12 hours later
International Date Line, East (IDLE)	180° E longitude, 12 hours later

stationary period. A period in which a planet appears to be motionless just before turning retrograde or direct in motion. When the planet is in its *station*. The Sun and Moon are never stationary.

Planet	Stationary Period
Mercury	1 day
Venus	2 days
Mars	3 days
Jupiter	5 days
Saturn	5 days
Uranus	6 days
Neptune	7 days
Pluto	7 days

See diagram under *retrograde motion.*

stellium. Satellitium. A cluster or group of four or more planets in one sign or house. Often the focal point of the horoscope.

succedent houses. The neutral of the mundane house, corresponding to the fixed signs: Second House (Taurus), Fifth House (Leo), Eighth House (Scorpio), Eleventh House (Aquarius).

Sun Sign. The sign of zodiac in which the Sun is located at any given time. The Sun Sign can be determined by knowing the day of the year, and is the basis for popular or newspaper astrology.

superior conjunction. See *combust.*

superior planets. Ponderous planets. Those planets whose orbits are on the other side of the Earth from the Sun: Mars, Jupiter, Saturn, Uranus, Neptune, and Pluto. See diagram under *solar system.*

symbols. The symbols of the signs and planets are composed of four basic shapes with the following meanings:

○ eternity; spirit; primal power
☉ beginning of emergence of spiritual power
) (soul
+ material world

Symbols of the signs and planets:

♈ Aries   ♋ Cancer
♉ Taurus   ♌ Leo
♊ Gemini   ♍ Virgo

♎︎ Libra
♏︎ Scorpio
♐︎ Sagittarius
♑︎ Capricorn
♒︎ Aquarius
♓︎ Pisces
☉ Sun
☽ Moon

☿ Mercury
♀ Venus
♂ Mars
♃ Jupiter
♄ Saturn
⚕ ♅ Uranus
♆ Neptune
♀ ♇ Pluto

Other symbols used in astrology:

☊ ascending node
☋ descending node
♂ ⊕ Earth
‖ parallel
⊕ Part of Fortune
☌ conjunction
⌁ vigintile
∨ quindecile
ⴸ semisextile
⊥ decile
∠ semisquare
⚹ sextile
Q quintile
□ square

⅌ tredecile
△ trine
sesquiquadrate
⊼ quincunx
± biquintile
☍ opposition
◯● New Moon
◯☽ second quarter
◯ Full Moon
◯☾ fourth quarter
✳ fixed star
◯ comet

synastry. The process of comparing two or more horoscopes interpreted in reference to the relationship between the people involved.

synodic. The period between two successive conjunctions of two planets.

synthesis. The art of combining the various and often contradictory influences in the horoscope in order to give a balanced interpretation of the whole chart.

syzygy. Yoking together. Three planets in a straight line, such as occurs between the Sun, Moon, and Earth during the new moon and full moon. Also, loosely, conjunctions and oppositions.

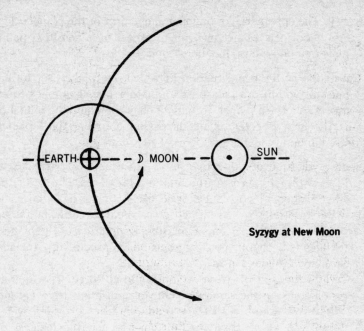

Syzygy at New Moon

T

table of diurnal planetary motion. Tables giving the distance a planet travels in a given period of time with reference to its daily motion.

tables of houses. Tables giving the signs and degree for the cusps of houses in a horoscope appropriate to the latitude of birth according to the sidereal time of birth.

tenancy. The location of a planet in a sign or house.

terms. Traditional subdivisions of the signs into five sections ruled by different planets, now largely in disuse.

testimony. Indications seen in a horoscope. The synthesis of several testimonies or arguments constitutes a *judgment*.

transit. The ephemeral, or ongoing, movement of the planets. The movement of a planet over, or in aspect to, a sensitive point, planet, or house cusp in a horoscope.

translation of light. A situation in which one planet, separating but still within orb of aspect to another planet, applies to an aspect to a third planet, forming a chain in which the influence of the first aspected planet is passed onto the third planet. Used in horary astrology.

trine. A division of the zodiac by 3. An aspect that is exact at 120°, with a 10° orb for the Sun and Moon, an 8° orb for the other planets. Two planets trine each other are in the same element; different quadruplicities (cardinal/mutable, mutable/fixed, fixed/cardinal); same polarity. The natures of the planets are blended, complementing each other, producing ease and harmony. A major aspect.

Grand trine: Planets trine each other in all three of the quadruplicities, in the same element, form a grand trine (grand fire trine, grand earth trine, grand air trine, or grand water trine). A grand trine can be too easy, causing laziness or boredom about matters pertaining to that element. When balanced by other aspects, it can be very beneficial.

triplicities. See *elements*.

U

unknown planets. Hypothetical planets. Eight symbolic indicators in Uranian astrology: Cupido, Hades, Zeus, Kronos, Appolon, Admetos, Vulkanus, and Poseidon. Also, possible actual undiscovered planets, some of which have been hypothesized as Trans-Pluto, Persephone, Lilith, Vulcan, and Arcturus, or Psyche.

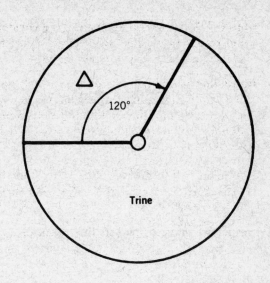

Trine

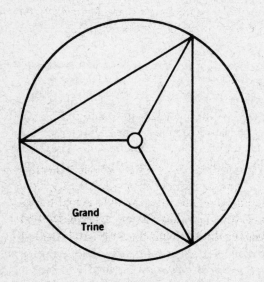

Grand
Trine

V

Vertex. The Vertex is an experimental point in the horoscope. It is calculated by subtracting the birth latitude from 90° to find the colatitude; noting the degree and sign upon the Fourth House cusp and regarding it as a Midheaven reference in the tables of houses; finding this reference under the Midheaven column in the tables of houses at the colatitude; noting the Ascendant listing for this reference. This new Ascendant becomes the Vertex.

vespertine. Stars or planets that set in the evening after the Sun, particularly the Moon (third quarter) and Mercury or Venus (occidental) when they appear in the evening. Opposite of *matutine*.

void of course. A situation in which a planet will form no more major aspects before leaving the sign in which it is tenanted. Most often applied to the Moon in horary astrology.

Z

Zenith. The point directly overhead. A line from any place to its Zenith would always be perpendicular to the plane of its horizon. Often incorrectly applied to the Midheaven. The Midheaven, being on the ecliptic, is south of the Zenith in the northern hemisphere. Opposite of *Nadir*. See diagram under *Nadir*.

zodiac. Tropical zodiac. Moving zodiac. Circle of Animals. The circle or band following the path of the ecliptic, extending about 9° on either side of it. Distance along the zodiac is measured in terms of *zodiacal longitude,* divided into twelve signs of 30° each, beginning with the vernal equinox point at 0° Aries.

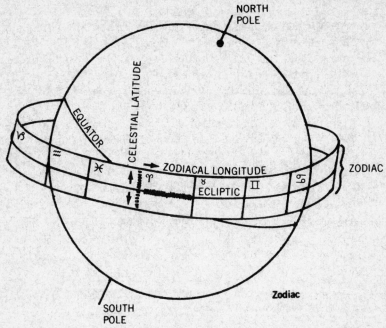

Distance perpendicular to the center of the zodiac, the *ecliptic,* is measured in terms of *ecliptical,* or *celestial, latitude,* in degrees north or south of the ecliptic. The Sun has no latitudes, as its path defines the ecliptic. See also *signs of the zodiac.*

References

DeVore, Nicholas. *Encyclopedia of Astrology.* New York: Philosophical Library, 1972.

Hone, Margaret E. *The Modern Text-Book of Astrology.* London: L. N. Fowler & Co., Ltd., 1951.

Jones, J. Allen. *Advanced Math for Astrological Students.* Hollywood, Ca.: Golden Seal Research Headquarters, 1968.

Mayo, Jeff. *The Astrologer's Astronomical Handbook.* London: L. N. Fowler & Co., Ltd., 1965.

Meyer, Michael R. *A Handbook for the Humanistic Astrologer*. Garden City, N.Y.: Doubleday/Anchor, 1974.

Moore, Marcia, and Mark Douglas. *Astrology: The Divine Science*. York Harbor, Me.: Arcane Publications, 1971.

Symbols and Signs. *The Astrology Annual Reference Book*. North Hollywood, Ca.: Symbols and Signs, annual.

Tyl, Noel. *Teaching and Study Guide to the Principles and Practice of Astrology*. Saint Paul, Minn.: Llewellyn Publications, 1976.

Williams, David. *Simplified Astronomy for Astrologers*. Washington, D.C.: American Federation of Astrologers.

Wilson, James. *Dictionary of Astrology*. New York: Samuel Weiser, 1974. (Originally published 1880.)

ath House,' Uranus. Core points to Aquarius and the Eleventh House.